Old-Fash

Garden
Wisdom

A FRIEDMAN/FAIRFAX BOOK

©2001, 2000 by Michael Friedman Publishing Group, Inc.

Library of Congress Cataloging-in-Publication data available upon request

ISBN 1-56799-767-8

Editor: Susan Lauzau
Art Director: Jeff Batzli
Production Manager: Camille Lee
Illustrations: ©Joanna Roy

3 5 7 9 10 8 6 4 2

For bulk purchases and special sales, please contact:
Friedman/Fairfax Publishers
Attention: Sales Department
15 West 26th Street
New York, New York 10010
212/685-6610   FAX 212/685-1307

Visit our website:
www.metrobooks.com

Disclaimer
While many herbal and home remedies have been used safely for years, inexperience can be dangerous.
Improper or excessive doses of certain herbs can cause allergic or even toxic reactions. For this reason,
the author has been conservative in describing uses. Neither the author nor the publisher
will be held responsible for any adverse reactions.

Old-Fashioned
Garden
Wisdom

Tips, Lore, and
Good Advice for Creating
a Beautiful, Healthy Garden

LARRY MAXCY

Illustrations by
JOANNA ROY

FRIEDMAN/FAIRFAX

PUBLISHERS

DEDICATION

This is for Carol, who knows the important questions and answers, and for my mother, Gertrude Maxcy, 1904-1999.

ACKNOWLEDGMENTS

My thanks to Teri Dunn, teacher, coach, and friend, who started the ball rolling years ago and who keeps it going. And thanks, too, to Crystal, Judy, Denise, and Polly, for their nuggets and tidbits, the gardeners at rec.gardens, and to my grandfather, Wilmer Stahl, who planted a seed a long time ago.

CONTENTS

INTRODUCTION

ardening is a modern way to satisfy an ancient human need. For millennia, people spent nearly all their time growing their food. They lived close to the soil and everyone was responsible for adding to the common storehouse. People like to be near plants. And plants, in turn, were necessary for there to be people, or communities, or even civilizations at all.

In his essay "How Flowers Changed the World" Loren Eiseley, archeologist, anthropologist, and philosopher, relates how the evolution of the flower, and the seed it produces and is produced from, provided the stored energy necessary for humans to have time for activities other than survival. Eiseley speculates about the primitive human, who, emerging from the forest, might have plucked a handful of grass seed and held it contemplatively:

> In that moment, the golden towers of man, his swarming millions, his turning wheels, the vast learning of his packed libraries, would glimmer dimly there in the ancestor of wheat, a few seeds held in a muddy hand. Without the gift of flowers and the infinite diversity of their fruits, man and bird, if they had continued to exist at all, would be today unrecognizable. Archaeopteryx, the lizard-bird, might still be snapping at beetles on a sequoia limb; man might still be a nocturnal insectivore gnawing at a roach in the dark. The weight of a petal has changed the face of the world and made it ours.

So when we plant our seeds and tend our flowers, we are connecting with our origins, affirming our friendly association with seeds and flowers and the plants that carry them. When we dig into warm soil and drop a seed into a furrow, we are just being human.

This book looks at some good old-fashioned gardening basics, without which no garden will succeed, and explores folk beliefs that have long governed gardening practices, such as astrological planting. It also gives advice on this and that, wanders about in various geographical regions, looks at useful and beautiful plants, hints, urges, and, I hope, entertains. Gardening may be a serious topic, but gardeners shouldn't be.

SOIL PRIMER

 oil is the natural place to start any discussion of gardening. It may seem too basic to mention, but your gardening success will depend in large part on the quality of your soil. Even if your soil starts out as pretty poor stuff, it can be improved. There are few places in the world that can boast naturally superior soil. Mostly, good soil is the result of good management and hard work.

WHAT IS SOIL, ANYWAY?

Soil is composed of mineral and organic components—bits of weathered rock, decomposed material from plants and animals, water, and, surprisingly, air. Rock weathers over a very long period to provide the basis for soil. Different rocks will turn into different materials. Soft shales eventually lead to clay, while sandstones crumble into sand. Weathered limestone makes fine soil, often slightly alkaline, while granites form acid soil. Organic matter provides humus, produced when plant tissue

breaks down and rots. Healthy soil is full of life—worms, fungi, and bacteria. These creatures all work together to break down organic material, mix and aerate the soil, add fertilizer, and balance the acid-alkali ratio.

All this geology may be of some academic interest to the home gardener, but the essential information is more specific—what is my soil like, should I test it, how can I improve it, and when can I work it in the spring? The following tips will give you some ideas about how best to care for your soil.

CHECKING SOIL DRAINAGE

To grow healthy plants, you will usually need soil that drains well but holds some moisture. If your soil is too sandy or too clayey, you will have to choose plants that thrive in that situation or amend the soil to change drainage patterns. Most garden soils are a combination of sand, silt, and clay, and there are a variety of tests that will accurately determine the specific amounts of each component in the soil. For most gardeners, though, the "drain test" gives enough information to work with.

This test is pretty simple—just dig a few holes about a foot (30cm) deep in your garden, spaced well apart. Fill each hole with water, and then check back every hour or so to see how the holes are draining. If the water disappears in less than an hour, you probably have sandy soil that drains too well. If the holes still have water standing in them after seven or eight hours, you have clay soil with poor drainage. If the water drains away in two to six hours, you have a good combination of soil materials with adequate drainage.

IMPROVING DRAINAGE

Heavy clay soils will drain better if you dig in plenty of peat moss, compost, or bagged organic soil amendments. These materials make the soil more friable, and excess water will drain away, even as the soil retains moisture in a form that plant roots can use.

TESTING FOR NUTRIENTS

You can quite easily test your soil for the nutrients it contains. This may be worthwhile to do in a new garden, but it isn't essential. Home soil test kits work reasonably well in determining the presence or absence of the main nutrients in the soil. These easy-to-use kits contain test tubes and a color chart—you simply place some soil in the test tube, add water, and check the results against the color chart provided.

Your local Agricultural Extension Service or a commercial soil-testing laboratory will give you a more complete and more accurate test, providing information on several nutrients and often making recommendations on how to improve any deficiencies. Check your local telephone book for the numbers—the government pages will have the number for the U.S. Department of Agriculture's Extension Service and the yellow pages will provide names and numbers for soil test laboratories.

IMPROVING YOUR SOIL

Soil can't be *too* good—healthy soil produces healthy plants. This seems obvious, but too often it's forgotten. Soil can have ample amounts of nitrogen, potassium, and phosphorous—all the important trace elements—and still plants won't grow well in it. The problem could be too much or too little water, or a pH level that is too high or too low. (See Fertilizing Wisely on page 10 and Changing the pH of Your Soil on page 11.) Lack of air is another reason for poor plant performance that is often overlooked. A lack of oxygen makes nutrients unavailable to plant roots, and soggy, oxygen-starved soil promotes the transformation of soil nitrates into nitrogen gas. Sadly, the nitrogen that could have nourished the plant leaks out of the soil.

The best materials for improving your garden's soil come from plants that have decayed or been composted. This plant matter can be tilled in, dug in by hand, or even left on the surface to rot (see Preparing a Garden Bed on page 27). It can be grown in place or hauled in (by dump truck if you have a big garden, by wheelbarrow if your garden is of more manageable dimensions). You can put it on in spring or autumn. It's a good idea to use some organic material for mulching during the growing season, and then leave it in place to "melt" into the soil during the garden's down time.

Each area of the country has locally available materials that are popular as soil improvers. (Well, perhaps I should say "most" areas. Deserts and mountaintops generally don't produce abundant organic material, and there is not usually enough to be used as soil conditioners.) Most gardeners have available a variety of amendments—following are a few of the most popular ones:

- redwood soil conditioner
- spoiled hay
- ground corn cobs
- sawdust
- cottonseed hulls
- shredded newspaper
- manure

FERTILIZING WISELY

Organic fertilizers are always the best choice for your garden. These fertilizers are derived from plants and animals—steer and chicken manure, blood meal, bone meal, brewery waste, cottonseed meal, and fish meal are prime examples of good organic fertilizers.

In the three numbers listed on fertilizer packages (called the NPK formula)—10-4-4, for instance—the first number listed refers to the fertilizer's nitrogen (N) content. The second refers to phosphorus (P) and the third to potassium (K). These are the primary nutrients essential for plant growth, although many other elements, called trace elements, are needed in minuscule amounts.

DETERMINING THE AMOUNT OF NITROGEN IN FERTILIZER

To determine the number of pounds of nitrogen (or any component, for that matter) in a bag of fertilizer, multiply the weight of the bag in pounds by the percentage of nitrogen. For example, if the bag weighs

50 pounds and the NPK formula is shown as 10-4-4, multiply 50 times 10 percent (translated into decimal form: .10). The answer is 5, so you know that the bag contains 5 pounds of nitrogen.

Changing the pH of Your Soil

The pH scale measures acidity and alkalinity, with 0 representing the most acidic and 14 the most alkaline. Seven, then, is the neutral point. Most plants grow best in a range close to neutral but a bit on the on the acid side, somewhere between 6 and 7. Some plants—azaleas, rhododendrons, and camellias, for example—prefer soil below 6.

Following are directions for altering the pH level in your soil. All are calculated for 100 square feet (9.3m^2) of garden area.

❦

To raise your soil pH by one point (for instance, from 5 to 6) add ground dolomitic limestone: use 8 pounds (3.6kg) for clay soil, 6 pounds (2.7kg) for loam, and 4 pounds (1.8kg) for sandy soil.

❦

To lower the pH level of your soil by one point (say from 8 to 7) add aluminum sulfate: 6 pounds (2.7kg) for clay soil, 6^1/$_2$ pounds for loam (2.9kg), and 2^1/$_2$ (1kg) pounds for sandy soil.

WORMS

Worms are the gardener's friend, and a good gardener will want to do everything possible to encourage worms to have large families. Amending the soil with organic matter (such as manure, decayed plant parts, even shredded newspapers) and keeping the soil from drying out completely are two of the best ways to encourage worms.

Worms break up heavy soil, turn dead plant material to fertilizer, devour lawn thatch, make holes in the soil that allow air and water to move through it, and in general work hard to improve your garden. Poor soil will not support many worms, but as soon as you begin to improve it the worms will start multiplying.

CONDITIONING THE SOIL WITH LEAVES

Now the big news. The best soil conditioner is leaves—your own, your neighbor's, and ones from the people down the street. With leaves you can make over-the-winter compost. In autumn, make a circular container several feet (meters) across using material such as chicken wire or snow fencing. The enclosing wire should be at least 4 feet (1.2m) tall. Fill the container with leaves, wetting them down several times as you add leaves. After six months, in early spring, you should have some wonderful soil in that container. Most of the leaves should have rotted away—any that didn't decompose completely can be dug or tilled into the soil, or even left in the container to continue breaking down.

A fast and easy way to make leaf mulch is by chopping the leaves with a power mower. Any mower will work. I have great success with a regular electric mower, which is less frustrating to work than the traditional gas model. If an electric mower gets clogged, it just stops and you release the power lever and unclog it. With a gas mower you have to go through the ritual of restarting. A riding mower also works well, and almost never clogs if the leaves are reasonably dry.

The chopped leaves break down quickly. I have left them on the lawn in the autumn, and can't find a trace of them on the surface by spring. They are easy to dig in around perennials or to pile up as a winter mulch. And there's a bonus—once shredded they don't blow around nearly as much.

Leaves from any type of tree work well as a winter mulch and soil improver. You might have heard that some leaves, such as oak, are acidic. They may be a little on the acidic side, but they will have had a very minor effect on soil by the time spring arrives. The same is true for black walnut leaves. Black walnut tree roots produce a substance toxic to other plants, a device intended to keep the ground around the tree clear. The leaves contain small amounts of the toxin, called juglone. Once the leaves have been composted for a time, or have weathered over the winter, their toxic properties become greatly diluted and they can be dug into the garden safely.

SOIL-IMPROVING MULCHES

All "organic" mulches improve the soil, mostly by decomposing into the ground and adding humus. Some popular ones are shredded bark, leaf mold, pine needles, sawdust, straw, and commercial compost. To prevent weeds, organic mulches should be used generously. At least 4 inches (10cm) of cover is necessary to prevent weed growth, and sometimes even very thick layers won't eliminate all weeds.

Even if you do get some weed growth, mulch keeps the soil loose and damp, so pulling the weeds is easy. And the weeds themselves, if they have not flowered and gone to seed, can be used as mulch. Just be sure the weed roots are not growing back into the soil. You can prevent this by breaking off the roots from the top.

❧

To the greatest extent possible, avoid leaving soil bare and exposed. Bare soil dries out in the sun and its humus content drops significantly. It becomes like concrete, and is difficult to work. At the other extreme, bare soil is vulnerable to being washed away by rain. Dried-out soil turns to dust, and wind scatters dust. Even a cover crop of weeds, if you pick them before they set seeds, is preferable to bare dirt.

COMPOSTING

FIRST, A REALITY CHECK

he best material for improving soil is compost, but there is a practical problem with compost. Every garden writer this century, and some before, recommends compost: the first thing you must do, the authoritarian voice says, is start a compost pile. It is garden gold. It can be used with all plants in any quantity. It fertilizes the plant, cools fevered soils, and feeds extended families of earthworms. All true. But there's a catch.

It's a whale of a lot of work to maintain a compost pile. The materials are heavy, and they must be stirred and mixed. The proper blend of green and brown, fresh and dry is not usually at hand at the same time. High temperature is crucial, and not always easy to attain or maintain. It's my guess that compost pile failures outnumber by far compost pile victories.

If you want to try your hand at composting, go ahead and do it. I'll even tell you how. But if you don't have a working compost pile, don't fret. It's not a moral failure. Millions of perfectly nice people have never made compost. Or rather, have never made a compost pile. Compost makes itself.

🌿

If you want compost and have been unwilling or unable to make a successful compost pile yourself, *buy* some compost. Or ground corn cobs. Or whatever is available and affordable. If you are in or near a rural area, manure is often available from farmers and ranchers at little or even no cost if you haul it yourself. And there may well be someone around with a thirty-year-old dump truck who will transport it for a reasonable fee.

🌿

Spoiled hay—that is, hay that has become unsuitable for use as animal feed, often because it got wet and fermented—is a wonderful mulch and soil conditioner, but it has become popular and that means it may be scarce.

🌿

If you have a local mushroom grower you're in luck. Commercial mushrooms are grown in a bed of fermented wheat straw and sand, with a little horse manure thrown in. This growing medium is "spent" as a mushroom producer after about three months, and is then sold. Mushroom compost doesn't contain much in the way of fertilizer, but it is unsurpassed as a soil conditioner. Four to 6 inches (10 to 15cm) dug into the top 12 inches (30cm) of your garden will greatly improve soil structure, aeration, water-holding capability, and drainage simultaneously, and even makes the soil look better.

🌿

While some garden sophisticates may chuckle at composted steer manure, I have found it to be a useful and effective soil conditioner, and it adds a little nitrogen, too. Regular use in arid areas can result in salt buildup, but this is not a problem in most of the country.

BUILDING A COMPOST PILE

First, build an enclosure or arrange a dedicated space for the pile. The enclosure can be fairly elaborate, made of wood and wire, cinder blocks, or welded wire. Or, it can be just a pile on the ground, uncontained. If you are building an enclosure, two things are important: the enclosure should be open at the bottom and it should have sides that allow air to get to the pile.

A good choice for a homemade bin is 12- or 14-gauge welded wire 4 feet (1.2m) high. A 12-foot (3.5m) length, formed into a circle with its ends fastened, will make a bin with a diameter of about 4 feet (1.2m). This makes one of the best compost enclosures when it comes to turning the pile, because you don't have to actually turn the material at all. Simply unfasten the ends and lift the wire away from the compost pile. Set up the wire circle near the original pile and transfer the composting materials from the pile to the new bin, thus "turning" it much more easily than if you had tried to move the bottom of the pile onto the top while keeping all the compost in the same place.

Similar to the wire bins discussed above, a cinder block enclosure (make sure to place the open ends of the cinder blocks toward the pile) can be built with a center "wall" so that the material can be put on one side and "turned" by forking it over to the other side every week or two.

COMMERCIAL COMPOST BINS

Compost bins are also available in kit form, and this is the easiest option for most people, especially if, like me, your carpentry skills are but faintly visible. Many of these kits have slots in the sides where you can insert a fork to help turn, or at least agitate, the decomposing material. Most of these compost bins are made of plastic, which doesn't gradually rot away along with the composting material.

Other commercial products include barrels or drums that spin on ball bearings. The gardener adds plant material, moistens it, and rotates the drum occasionally. While they are more expensive, these tumbling composters work well and quickly, providing acceptable compost in several weeks.

What Goes Into a Compost Pile?

Whether or not your compost pile is enclosed, the basics of constructing the pile are the same. The pile should contain a balance of carbon, in the form of "brown" material, and nitrogen, which is usually "green" material.

Brown material includes leaves, dry grass clippings, and dried-up weeds (not those that have flowered or seeded), pine needles, sawdust, straw, and old hay. If you don't have enough brown material (which often happens when composting in the spring), shredded newspaper works just fine.

Green stuff can be fresh grass clippings, fresh manure (sometimes green in color, sometimes not!), pea and bean plants that have stopped producing but are still green, weeds without seeds, and rich sources of nitrogen such as blood meal, soybean meal, and kitchen vegetable scraps.

A word of warning: never add meat, fats or oils, bones, or pet feces. Meat and bones will attract rats and other undesirables, while pet feces can (though this is rare) contain parasites or disease organisms.

17

BUILDING A "FAST COMPOST" PILE

This method will give you good compost in several weeks, but as you can see, it takes a lot of effort. Fast composting (also called hot composting) is the typical method used, and is the one generally promoted by compost gurus. (See Slow Composting below for a low-maintenance approach to composting.)

To build a fast compost pile:

1. Dump about 6 inches (15cm) or so of brown material into your compost bin or onto the spot where your pile will be housed.

2. Top the brown material with about 3 inches (7cm) of green.

3. Repeat steps 1 and 2. Note that if you have very "carbony" material for the brown part—sawdust, shredded newspapers, or wood shavings—add extra nitrogen in the form of manure, blood meal, or grass clippings to speed decomposition.

4. Gently wet the material as you add it, adding enough moisture so the entire pile is just damp but not dripping.

5. Finally, add some soil to give your pile necessary microorganisms such as bacteria.

The pile should begin to heat up quickly. If it doesn't, try adding additional nitrogen. Turn the pile occasionally, every week or so. You should have usable compost in about a month.

"SLOW COMPOSTING"

Slow, or cold, composting takes a lot longer to produce usable compost, but it represents a lot less work for the gardener.

A cold compost pile is an aggregation of plant material that is decomposing slowly. You can add material to it at any time. You should probably loosen it up from time to time using a pitchfork, but you need not turn the pile completely. The proportion of green and brown materials is not especially important, as they will all break down if you wait long enough. In slow composting, the nitrogen-carbon balance is not as critical, since you are not relying on generated heat to speed up decomposition.

The best time to start a slow compost pile is in the autumn, when a lot of plant material and leaves are available. If you live where the ground does not freeze, the pile will continue to be active through the winter, and a good product may be available by spring planting time. If you live in a cold climate, the pile will doze through the winter and reactivate as the weather warms. It should finish about the time the leaves from the trees are falling again.

If your lazy compost pile is just a heap on the ground, it should be covered if your climate is rainy, since you don't want the pile to get soggy. An old tarp, or even black plastic held down with something heavy, is suitable. The cover can be left off in good weather or if you want to wet the pile in a soft rain. Make sure your pile is rounded at the top so that water runs off the heap. A pile with a depression at its top will catch too much water.

TRENCH COMPOSTING

Trench composting is an easy method, and one with great appeal for neat freaks. For this method, dig a trench about a foot (30cm) deep in the garden. This can be done at any time of year, but note that material is most available at harvest time. Line the trench with plant material—kitchen scraps, dead weeds (but no seeds), any plant material at all—and then fill in the trench with the removed topsoil. The next year, plant vegetables in the trench row; the roots of the vegetables will reach down into the buried material that has rotted into compost.

Worms consider anything you trench as a wonderful gift, and will do their best to break it down, turning it into rich worm castings. A good approach is to rotate your vegetable rows and paths from year to year: the first year use the covered trench for paths, then plant in that area the next year, even as you bury plant material for composting below the current paths.

ORDERING PLANTS AND SEEDS

LOCAL NURSERIES VERSUS MAIL-ORDER SUPPLIERS

If you have been gardening for a while and have ordered any garden supplies by mail, you are probably receiving lots of catalogs. Ordering plants and seeds by mail can greatly increase the scope of what you can grow. But keep this in mind—it's a good policy for you to get as many plants as possible from your local garden center or nursery. First, if something goes wrong, you have an immediate remedy at hand. Plants will be fresher, in many cases, and planting advice is available from trained nursery staff. Most garden merchants, especially those based locally, will be happy to order special plants or seeds for you.

Still, no garden center can supply everything you might wish to have. Some plants will be available only by mail order. Also, mail-order suppliers may offer discounts if you order large quantities, especially for items such as spring bulbs. Some catalogs contain excellent gardening advice written by the experts who run the business, and many have customer service representatives who can answer questions or handle difficulties.

❧

Winter is the traditional time to sit down with your catalogs, ignore the weather outside, and let your mind wander through the many possibilities the new season will bring. Some people sketch out their garden plot, designing their gardens on paper. Others prefer to develop a mental picture of what their ideal garden will look like. Both types of gardener will almost certainly order too many seeds.

Ordering seeds and plants by mail is a pleasant and safe experience. Plants I've ordered have always arrived healthy and with good directions for care and planting. I have been careful to choose sources I have had some experience with, or which have been recommended by people I trust. I have shied away from gaudy catalogs, especially ones with illustrations of flowers with improbable colors and blooms of unbelievable size. In most cases, catalog photographs show you what the plant will look like at a mature stage when well grown, but that's certainly not cheating. See page 150 for a list of reliable mail-order suppliers.

SPECIALTY GROWERS

Ordering plants by mail gives you the chance to buy from specialty growers—usually, these are small operations run by the owner. You will find ads for these suppliers in the classified section at the back of gardening magazines, and in my view these are excellent places to pick up real treasures. Since these nurseries specialize in a particular plant or a specific type of gardening, the owners are experts at growing the plants they carry. There are specialty suppliers for almost every plant, from cacti to fruit trees to hardy perennials. There are also specialty suppliers for niche areas of gardening, such as water gardening, xeriscaping, and growing heirloom varieties.

SEED SUPPLIERS

Seeds have their own network of growers. The large national companies, such as Burpee and Park, are not only reliable, they carry a wide assortment of seeds at good prices. The same holds true for smaller and regional firms.

One of the most unusual and interesting seed suppliers is J.L. Hudson, who has run a specialty seed business for many years. His catalog is a treasury of useful information and biting essays on various aspects of ethnobotany. All the seeds he carries are open-pollinated, which means that they are not patented and that the seeds will grow true if harvested and saved for planting the following year. He carries some seeds no one else lists, including a selection of vegetable and flower seeds from the high mountains of Mexico, grown for centuries by the Zapotec people, called People of the Clouds by neighboring tribes. Mr. Hudson is an old-fashioned businessman; he has no telephone and accepts no credit cards, but is happy to honor your check. His catalog is a dollar; there is no better bargain in gardendom.

STARTING SEEDS

STARTING YOUR OWN SEEDS

ne easy way to get into some serious gardening, without needing to know a whole lot or spending tons of money on specialized equipment, is to start your own seeds indoors in the spring. You can get a much wider variety of plants that way—both a larger selection of colors and types than is usually available in the retail market and some rare plants not found at local garden stores. Seeds of unusual plants often aren't any harder to germinate than those of common plants.

Seeds are amazing little things. When you consider it, plants have a much more evolved system of reproducing themselves than humans do. Often, the seeds of a plant can sit on a shelf for several years and still do what they're supposed to do when the time comes. Some seeds of the sacred lotus of China, known to be hundreds of years old, were discovered a few years ago. Scientists in California germinated the seeds, which grew into perfect plants. Mammals, by contrast, have fragile and closed systems that are, comparatively speaking, grossly inefficient. While we may prefer the process, the method is random and the outcome uncertain. With seeds, the outcome is known. A seed—put in an acceptable medium, moistened, and given the proper temperature and light—will fulfill its destiny every time.

INGREDIENTS FOR HOME GERMINATION

To germinate seeds at home all you need is a germinating mix and containers. The best mix is a soilless one. I prefer milled sphagnum moss (not peat moss), vermiculite, and perlite, in proportions of 4-2-1. Ordinary garden soil put into a container will become bricklike, and is almost certain to contain organisms that will result in the tragedy of "damping off," a fungal disease fatal to seedlings. While soil can be sterilized at home by baking it in the oven (a disgusting, stinking practice) or with the addition of fungicides, it's best to avoid using it.

Milled sphagnum moss is finely ground moss, tan in color, that makes a good basic seed bed. Vermiculite (mica that has been treated by heat and made to expand) holds water and gives body to the moss. It also contains a touch of magnesium and potassium, essential to seedling development. Perlite is volcanic ash, and holds water on its surface. It tends to float to the top of the mix, and should be used sparingly. I like to use a bit because it lightens the vermiculite, which can otherwise clump.

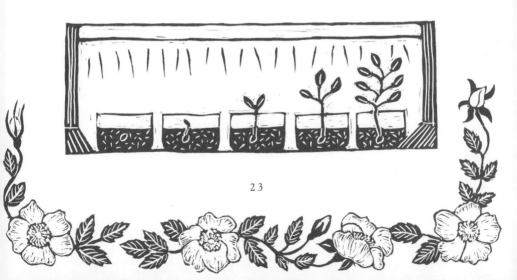

As a container for my seedlings, I use a propagating kit that contains a Styrofoam grid, a capillary mat, and a water reservoir. The grid is open at the top and bottom, and holds the soilless mix; a seed is planted in each compartment of the grid. The grid rests on the capillary mat. This system allows you to add enough water to the reservoir to last a week or so, and you can therefore leave the setup to do its thing without constant attention.

Seedlings can successfully be grown in cell packs, fitted into a tray. Water can be added to the tray, and will be absorbed through the drainage hole in the cell pack. Whatever method you use, it is far better to water from the bottom, allowing the water to be slowly absorbed by the mix. Watering from the top will disturb the seeds, crush tiny seedlings, and sometimes even wash them out.

Getting the Right Light

Some seeds require light for germination, while others require darkness. Most don't care much one way or the other. If the seeds require light, the seed packet or the catalog from which the seeds were purchased will provide this information. If a seed needs light to germinate, it should be sowed either on the surface of the soilless mix or covered just barely with the mix, so that some light gets through to the seed.

If darkness is required for the seeds to germinate (pansy seeds are an example), cover them well with the growing medium and then either keep the container in a dark place or cover it with several thicknesses of newspaper. You do have to be careful to watch their progress, for as the seedlings emerge they should quickly be moved into the light.

Light, in gardener's terms, refers to ordinary, diffuse daylight. Dark means low light, not necessarily pitch blackness. For example, my seed-starting endeavors take place in my pantry, which has a door that is usually open but no windows or bright lights, and this works out fine.

For seedlings that need to germinate in darkness, check the seed trays every day or so to see if any shoots are coming up. When you do see the first shoots, which will probably be little and white, transfer the entire tray to a well-lit spot, but don't set them in direct sun. The shoots will green up in a day or two, and the seeds that haven't yet sprouted will germinate with no problem. Seeds make a root before generating a top, so all the seeds have probably already germinated, though they may not all have started top growth.

TEMPERATURE

Most seeds will germinate well at room temperature, 65° to 75°F (18° to 24°C). If cooler temperatures are required (rarely will higher temperatures be needed) put the container in a spot that is a little cooler than your living area. A closet with an outside wall, a garage, a basement, or the space beneath a porch can serve as a germination room—just make sure that the temperature in the space doesn't drop below 50°F (10°C), or the seeds will suffer.

THINNING THE SEEDLINGS

Once all the seeds have germinated, you may have too many seedlings or you may have several clumps where a lot of seeds fell. In this case, use a small scissors to snip off excess seedlings. I know, it feels like snipping off your children, but this procedure is necessary to ensure that the seedlings you have left will grow into sturdy plants.

FERTILIZING SEEDLINGS

Since the soilless mix used as a growing medium for most seeds has almost no nutrients, you should fertilize once your seedlings get started. I use a balanced (20-20-20) liquid fertilizer, added to the water that keeps the plants moist from the bottom. You don't need much fertilizer— think baby food, bland and mild. I keep a little fertilizer in the water, but if the plants start to get leggy it could be a sign that the seedlings are getting too rich a dose. Another reason for legginess is insufficient light.

PROVIDING ENOUGH AIR

Note that moving air promotes bushy seedlings, so if you are keeping the plants indoors use a fan to stir up the air, but don't let the fan blow directly on the tiny seedlings. If your plants are living out of doors, natural breezes and winds will, of course, take care of this for you. The moving air seems to strengthen the stems, making the plant sturdy and stocky, a good thing at this stage.

HARDENING OFF

If your indoor seedlings are destined to be planted in the garden but have not yet spent time outdoors, they will need to be "hardened off." This means simply that the seedlings will need a period of gradual adjustment to outdoor conditions—sun, wind, night cold, and midday heat. Begin by taking your flat of seedlings out and leaving it in the sun for a short time, no more than an hour. Gradually increase the time by an hour or so each day until you are leaving the plants out all day. They will be ready to go into the ground after about a week. If you work all day and can't get home to move the seeds outdoors and back in, do the best you can. The point is to provide a transition period so the plants can acclimate to full sun, rather than exposing them to a long day of hot sun after a protected life indoors.

TRANSPLANTING SEEDLINGS INTO THE GARDEN

When it comes time to transplant the seedlings into the garden, have the soil already prepared. Garden soil should have been dug and loosened, and then raked level. Amendments and fertilizer should have been added (remember to keep the fertilizer at low concentrations). (See Preparing the Garden Bed on page 27 and Fertilizing Seedlings on page 25.)

Lift the seedlings gently out of their birth containers with a small fork, either a remnant from an old set or a plastic picnic model. Push the fork straight down on one side of the container and lever up the seedling, preserving as much of the rootball as you can. This should actually be fairly easy, for if the plant has been well grown in a germinating mix it should have a good-size rootball.

If you are transferring the seedling to a decorative planter, put some potting mix in the bottom of the container and place the seedling rootball in the pot. Gently add potting mix to cover the rootball, making sure that the little stem is above the  potting soil. The potting soil should be a bit below the top of the pot so that you can add water without causing an overflow.

If you are transplanting your seedlings into the garden, do it on a cloudy day or late in the day when the sun has lost its intensity. While your plants should be used to the sun after the hardening off period, sitting all day near the top of the soil can be very drying. Water the plants well and cover the dirt with a mulch, either compost, a soil conditioner, or hay. Don't water again for a week or so, unless you have drying wind or especially hot weather. I find plants establish themselves best if they are well watered when they are planted and then left alone for a little while.

Preparing Garden Beds

Tilling or Digging?

here are two methods for turning soil over in spring. You can either use a spade and spading fork, and dig using muscle power, or you can use a rototiller, which also requires a fair amount of muscle power. A rototiller can be a necessity when you are first starting a garden and need to break up turf or a mass of established weeds. Tilling with machinery is certainly a whole lot easier than digging the whole garden with a spade. On the other hand, rototilling can damage the soil if it is over-done. Overworking—tilling to the point where the soil gets powdery—destroys soil structure and makes for less-healthy plants.

❧

If you have a large garden and need to use a rototiller for your planting beds, it's common practice to till twice—once in spring to prepare and once in autumn to break up the soil, leaving it rough for winter. The autumn tilling will also expose any overwintering grubs to birds. In addition, tilling is the most efficient way to incorporate amendments and fertilizers into the soil, especially in a large garden.

If you have been improving your soil for years and have a rich and soft loam, you may prefer to dig manually to prepare the garden at the beginning of the year. Whenever possible, I choose this method. There is a deep psychological satisfaction that comes with working the soil by hand. But it can definitely be hard on the back.

DO YOU NEED A ROTOTILLER?

Rototillers are expensive, and they require care. Tines wear out and must be replaced, and the engine needs spring tuneups and oil changes, as well as late-season winterizing, all of which costs time and money. For most gardeners, it makes sense to rent a tiller once or twice a year. But if you have a large garden or will be bringing new areas into culti-vation over a period of time, and will be using the tiller as a cultivator throughout the year, you may want to invest in your own.

❧

There are two styles of tillers, those with tines in the front and those with tines is the rear. Those with front tines are fine for working an established garden, tilling in some winter weeds, or creating a new seedbed. For heavier tilling, especially if you need to break up turf or hard ground that has not been worked recently, you must use a tiller with the tines in the rear. The balance on these tillers is much better for heavy work, and the tines will tend to pull themselves down, exactly what you want to happen. Rear-tine tillers are generally more expensive, but may ultimately be the better buy.

❧

If you invest in a tiller of your own, you will not only have the flexibility of using it whenever you like, you might also consider renting yourself out to till other people's gardens. If you need tilling done, check the local want ads, bulletin boards at supermarkets, and notices at garden centers. You may find someone willing to do your tilling for not much more than you would pay to rent a machine, and you will also get that person's expertise as part of the deal.

PLANTING ADVICE

PLANTING CONTAINERIZED PLANTS

Following are a few tips on how to handle the plants you bring home in containers, especially fairly large ones that have been in cans for quite a while.

An old gardening cliché advises you to put a one-dollar plant in a ten-dollar hole, and that about sums up my advice, too. Dig a hole that is at least twice as deep and twice as wide as the dimensions of the container where the plant currently resides. If you have rich, loamy soil in your garden, you won't need to add anything at all. If, however, you are like most of us, you'll need to do a bit of soil improvement to give your new plants their best chance. Mix the native soil with compost, your favorite soil conditioner, and maybe even a bit of well-aged manure. Make the sides of the hole rough and irregular—plant roots prefer an easy transition between the soil you have enriched and the surrounding dirt rather than a smooth side that defines the line.

Remove the plant and its rootball from the container and shake the rootball carefully to get rid of loose potting soil. Spread the roots apart gently and set the plant on mounded soil in the bottom of the planting hole. You'll want the plant's crown to be at the same level in the soil that it was in its pot. Fill in around the plant, firming the soil gently, then water it well. Old-timers call this process "muddying in"—it's a way of making sure that the plant roots come into full contact with the soil and that any air pockets are filled in.

Mulch around the new plant and let the plant settle in undisturbed. If the weather is especially hot or very windy, make sure the soil doesn't dry out, but note that a little drying of the first inch or two (2.5–5cm) of surface soil is fine. Overwatering is more dangerous and much more likely.

If the plant and rootball don't slide out of the container easily, water the plant thoroughly, wait fifteen minutes, and try again. Try tapping sharply on the bottom of the can. If the plant still refuses to budge, you can be pretty sure it has been left in the can far too long, is rootbound, and will need a little extra tenderness.

If a containerized plant is rootbound, use tin snips or wire cutters to open the sides of the can or plastic container, and pull it away from the plant. If the roots are a clotted mass, and they probably are if you had to cut the container, take a very sharp knife and slice downward on the rootball, making four or five cuts from top to bottom and letting the knife go about an inch (2.5cm) into the massed roots. Then plant as you would any container-grown plant.

COMPANION PLANTING

THE BASIS FOR COMPANION PLANTING

I t has been taken as a matter of faith since ancient times that certain plants do well in the presence of certain other plants; conversely, close proximity of certain plants is said to be bad for one or both of them. In modern times chemists have added some scientific underpinnings to various of these folk beliefs. Chemists now know, for instance, that marigolds produce a chemical in their roots that is toxic to harmful soil nematodes. The effect was known long ago; the reason has been discovered only recently. The study of plant chemical warfare, known as allelopathy, has begun to clarify specific interactions. The agent in black walnut trees that acts as an herbicide to other plants, thus keeping the area around the trees plant-free, has been identified and named juglone, taken from *juglans*, the botanical name for walnut.

Other plant interactions are less direct. Some plants attract insects that attack other plants, especially if the plants are in the same family. One example is the carrot rust fly, which goes after not only carrots but also the related celery, dill, parsley, and others. It even attacks Queen Anne's lace, from which the modern-day carrot was developed in the seventeenth century.

Other "companion" plants may serve an entirely different purpose. Borage, it is said, is friendly with tomatoes, and should have a place in your tomato patch. The real reason tomatoes like borage is that the herb is a powerful bee attractor, and the more bees around to pollinate the plants, the better the tomato yield.

How did such beliefs originate and persist? One wonders. Probably, a gardener noticed that one year, when his beans were planted next to his corn, both crops did well. He told his neighbors about this amazing phenomenon, and they spread the word further.

But it was probably by chance that the original grower's beans were planted on the south side of his corn. Had they been planted on the north side, the corn would have shaded the beans, and most likely this would have resulted in a poor bean crop. Beans can capture nitrogen from the air and transfer it to the soil. Corn needs lots of nitrogen to grow well. So, beans planted on the sunny side of corn might be the best of both worlds—the beans get the sun and the corn gets the extra nitrogen.

❧

According to companion planting philosophy, carrots are not supposed to be comfortable when planted close to parsley or dill. Well, there's a connection here. All three—carrot, dill, and parsley—are members of the celery family (Apiaceae). Do these relatives attract the same bugs? Quite possibly. For example, the carrot rust fly, which feeds on the carrot root, also feeds on celery. Putting the two plants together just simplifies life for the bug.

❧

Some specific plant chemicals are known to have beneficial effects for their companion plants. The fragrant varieties of marigolds (some people would say the stinking varieties) exude a chemical from their roots that kills the nematodes called eelworms present in many gardens. Marigolds will also keep the numbers of cucumber beetles down in plantings of cucumbers, zucchini, and melons.

❧

Pot-marigolds, or calendulas, attract the flying adult beetles of wireworms to their blossoms. I spent hours last summer killing the beetles, which appeared to find the calendula blossoms completely intoxicating, and were easily tapped off and smashed.

🌿

Garlic is another useful plant, reputed to have a killing effect on aphids, particularly those on roses. Place some garlic plants throughout your garden, rather than growing them in isolation, and you should reduce any aphid population. Garlic also has other uses in the companion planting world—it's supposed to be effective against fruit tree borers and, it is reported, Japanese beetles. The gardener just needs to plant a few cloves under the fruit tree.

🌿

Sometimes the aim of a companion planting is to separate plants or establish barriers around them. Tansy, it is said, will repel cabbage worms, and thus should be inter-planted between rows of cabbages.

🌿

Tansy is effective in keeping ants out of the house if planted around doorways. Cucumbers will keep ants away if they are coming up from underneath the house, so if you are having ant problems, consider planting a cucumber vine or two alongside the house, especially near a door.

🌿

Chives will repel aphids, so plant them throughout the garden, among flowers as well as vegetables. Rosemary may keep away the cabbage butterfly, which lays the eggs that turn into the cabbage looper, and nasturtiums are known to repel harlequin bugs in broccoli.

🌿

One technique that will be very effective in reducing damage from insects and soil pests is to plant with variety in mind—don't segregate the garden into a carrot area and a lettuce area and a bean area, but rather plant short rows of this and that. Put in lots of different types of plants and bad bugs will have a tougher time finding just what they want. Note one exception, though—corn must be planted in a block to ensure good pollination.

ASTROLOGICAL PLANTING

PLANTING BY THE MOON

lanting different crops according to the phases of the moon has been practiced for thousands of years. Ancient peoples ascribed many powers to the moon; the moon was such a dominant feature of the natural world, they figured, it must be an important force in nature. Its effect on the tides has long been known, if not perfectly understood. It follows, then, that agriculture—originally the occupation of almost all humans—would be affected by the phases of the moon, as well as by the signs of the zodiac.

The basic premise, with many corollaries, is that plants that have their edible parts above ground do best if planted when the moon is waxing, that is, growing from the new moon to the full moon. Plants

with their edible parts beneath the ground, on the other hand, do best when planted during the waning moon, as it passes from full moon to new moon. Annuals, according to astrological planting practices, are optimally planted during the waxing moon, while perennials and bulbs should be planted during the waning period.

PLANTING ACCORDING TO THE ZODIAC

The above section outlines the basic philosophy of planting by the moon; the reality is much more complicated. Most people think of the signs of the zodiac as related to the sun. The classic pickup line "What's your sign?" alluded to the sun sign beneath which a person was born— thus a person might refer to him- or herself as a Gemini or an Aquarius, for instance.

The gardener's zodiacal signs are those of the moon. Each day of the year is ruled by a sign of the zodiac, determined by the zodiacal con- stellation that is most prominent in the sky on that day. Thus, it will be said that the moon is in Scorpio or Virgo. Each sign has its own specific attributes with regard to horticulture, so in astrological planting, not only the phase of the moon but also the zodiacal designation of the day is important. The moon moves through the entire zodiac every month. Generally it takes two or three days for the moon to move from one sign to another. Calendars that show the details for each day may be pur- chased in shops specializing in astrology and New Age merchandise. Fisherman's guides will also carry this information, as will some almanacs.

Does astrological gardening work? Is there a difference in the plants? I suppose that in one sense it does make a difference. If you are following an established plan and paying additional attention to the garden because of it, the garden may well be the better for the added care. If you believe in your magic, you may establish some sort of influ- ence. So does that mean it works? Well, as the saying goes, if it works for you....

The astrological year begins in early spring with Aries and continues through Pisces, at the end of winter. This makes more sense for a gardener than the Roman calendar, which begins January 1, in the dead of winter.

❦

The twelve signs of the zodiac are Aries the ram, Taurus the bull, Gemini the twins, Cancer the crab, Leo the lion, Virgo the virgin, Libra the balance, Scorpio the scorpion, Sagittarius the archer, Capricorn the goat, Aquarius the water bearer, and Pisces the fish.

❦

Parts of the body are associated with each sign, and influence astrological gardening as well. Aries is associated with the head, Taurus with the neck, Gemini with the arms, Cancer with the breast, Leo with the heart, and Virgo with the bowels. Libra is the sign of beauty, and Scorpio of the genitals. Sagittarius is associated with the thighs, Capricorn with the knees, Aquarius with the legs, and Pisces with the feet.

The specific connections between the body parts and gardening is somewhat obscure in astrological gardening. While each astrological sign "rules" a body part, and each sign is felt to have specific characteristics applying to gardening and plant growth, the two do not always meet, except in tenuous ways.

One folk tale warns against planting potatoes during the influence of Pisces, associated with feet, for fear the potatoes will develop unsightly toe-like knobs.

On the other hand, the signs paired with the lower extremities, Capricorn and Pisces, are considered favorable for rooting cuttings and planting bareroot trees.

Gemini controls the vascular system of plants, and sowing under this sign can result in unnaturally tall, weak plants.

Scorpio, the sign of the genitals, is an especially good time to plant for seeds and abundant fruit. It is also a good influence for transplanting, a process that mimics regeneration and rebirth.

The astrological sign considered most fruitful is Cancer, and it is felt to be the best sign for planting. It is also a water sign, favorable for irrigation. The body part connected here is the breast, with its connotations of nourishment and abundance.

❧

The most fruitful, productive signs to plant under are Cancer, Scorpio, and Pisces, followed by Taurus and Capricorn, and then Libra, Sagittarius, and Aquarius.

❧

Various crops are said to be influenced by their favored signs of the zodiac. A day in Taurus, an earth sign, is the time to plant root crops, especially if fast growth is desired. Good corn will come if you plant when the moon is in Scorpio. Libra days are flower days, since it is the sign of beauty. And it isn't only ornamental flowers that benefit; vegetables with flower parts that are eaten, such as broccoli, are helped by a Libra moon-sign planting.

❧

Leo, on the other hand, is a barren sign. Cut your grass in Leo, and it won't grow as fast. Pesky and persistent blackberry vines (are there any other kind?) are best rooted out and destroyed under the eye of Leo. Gemini is another barren sign, good for grass cutting, weeding, and cultivating. Surprisingly, melon seeds do well if planted in Gemini, but that's about it for planting. It's a good time to harvest, though, a trait all the barren signs share. Other barren signs are Aries and Virgo.

❧

The moon plays a major part in the astrological belief system. For example, consider cucumbers. Cucumbers are pollinated by insects, and it is believed that during the periods of bright moonlight the insects frolic and carouse all night, and are thus too tired during the day to pollinate. So, plan for your cucumbers to flower when the moon is dark and insects are getting a good night's sleep. In favorable weather cucumbers will flower in about a month, so plants started in the dark of the moon will bloom in the dark of the moon.

Corn is affected by the moon as well. In the lunar planting scenario, the last planting of corn should be made in early summer, timed so that the ears will be developing when the moon is new. The ears of corn will grow up, trying to capture the new moon. In that position the silks will be more easily pollinated by falling pollen. If the ears see the full moon they will cling closely to the stalk in fear, and pollination will be incomplete.

Herbs are thought to be greatly influenced by the moon. All should be planted in the first or second quarter. The important consideration is what you expect from the plants. If you are growing them for hardiness, plant under Taurus in the first quarter. For flowers, plant on a first-quarter Libra day, and for large numbers of leaves plant under Cancer, Virgo, or Pisces. Seeds will be most plentiful if planted on a Capricorn day in the first or second quarter.

Many people have for years grown alfalfa and bean sprouts for their health-strengthening properties. These, too, are affected by the moon sign that rules the day they are started. They will grow a little faster during days of the waxing moon. Days of the water signs—Pisces, Cancer, and Scorpio—are best for plant growth, a characteristic that applies to sprouts growing in a jar in the kitchen as well as to sprouts growing in the garden.

PLANT LORE

ecause plants and people lived in close association for millennia, a vast body of folklore arose around growing things.

HERBAL LORE

Herbs have long been used to enhance health and heal bodily ills, and have recently enjoyed a renaissance. Not surprisingly, their mysterious curative powers have made herbs the center of many legends and folk beliefs. Following are a few.

Legend has it that basil will not perform properly unless the gardener curses the plant soon after it sprouts. A tip—give it to your basil good, and it will reward you!

Lavender rubbed on the head of a young girl is supposed to keep her a virgin until she marries. And if you have any lavender left, put it in the closet to repel clothes-eating moths.

Mint (*Mentha* spp.) is the stuff of folklore. It is known to have been used in religious rites by the Assyrians five thousand years ago. The Greeks tell us that mint is the result of a jealous fit by the goddess Persephone, wife of Pluto and daughter of Demeter, the grain

goddess. Persephone believed her husband had fallen in love with the beautiful nymph Menthe, and, being a goddess, had the power to take decisive action. She changed Menthe into a plant that would grow where it would be stepped on and crushed. This was unlucky for the lovely Menthe, but her loveliness has been preserved for us in the delightful fragrance of mint.

St. John's wort (*Hypericum* spp.) has become popular as a natural tranquilizer, and is known to reduce pain and inflammation. But don't let sheep or cows eat it—the herb causes a dangerous phototoxic reaction, especially in light-skinned animals. Some herbalists caution that light-skinned people, too, could be affected. Wort, by the way, is Old English for "plant."

GARDEN FOLK WISDOM

In China it was a common practice to give two heavenly bamboo (*Nandina* spp.) plants as wedding presents. The bride and groom would plant the bamboo, one plant at the front door and one at the back. If the couple had disagreements, each would go to a plant and talk it out with the bamboo before talking to each other. The act of speaking to the plants allowed the couple to calm down and think clearly, and thus they were in a better position to resolve their dispute peacefully.

Old wisdom tells us that it is bad luck to thank someone for a gift plant, for if you do the plant won't thrive.

Gazing balls, shiny spheres with a mirror finish, have become popular again as garden ornaments, reviving a practice that goes back to the seventeenth century in England. While today they are used decoratively, these shiny objects originally had a different use: they were intended to preserve plants from wicked witches who came to steal the garden's choice plants. Attracted to the shiny balls, the witches would look into the mirrored surface. Disgusted by their own gruesome appearance, they quickly left the garden empty-handed.

40

Native Americans called the vital plants corn, beans, and squash "The Three Sisters," and often planted them together. The corn provided climbing stalks for the beans; in turn the beans added nitrogen to the soil, which corn uses heavily. The squash shaded the earth, keeping down weeds and serving as a trap for harmful insects by attracting the insects away from the more vulnerable corn.

Several plants have been tried as mosquito repellents. Reports on effectiveness are mixed, but two that may work are lemon verbena (*Aloysia triphylla*, a.k.a. *Lippia citriodora*) and lemon-scented pelargonium (*Pelargonium crispum*).

Orange bergamot carried in a wallet is said to attract money.

SEX IN THE GARDEN

 t's not surprising that a large body of folklore revolves around planting and fertility. Several generations ago, and for millennia before that, food didn't come from the supermarket. You raised it yourself, and the survival of your family in the year to come depended to a great extent on what sort of harvest you had. A farmer naturally looked for as much help as he could get. There were no county extension agents then, but there was tried-and-true magic, ritualistic methods that increased the chances for a good harvest.

The folklore chronicler Vance Randolph recounts many instances in nineteenth- and early-twentieth-century America of farmers planting their crops while naked, making love in newly sown fields at night, and other practices anthropologists might describe as fertility rites.

41

The English practice of sitting naked on soil to test whether it is warm enough to plant crossed the Atlantic and is still practiced in some mountain communities today. A similar practice developed separately among eastern Native Americans. In Iroquois societies women did the planting; when the planting season drew near the women would "kidnap" a young man, strip him, and sit him on a bare patch of garden. A shivering lad meant it was still too cold to plant.

❧

In the Ozarks, turnips are planted on the feast day of St. James, July 25. There is even a little poem to remind farmers: Plant 25 July, wet or dry.

❧

Human sexual energies were long believed to be transferable to plants. In some cultures, designated couples made love at the time of planting in order to give the seeds increased vigor. And in many places, planting done by a pregnant woman is expected to be especially successful. Fruit trees planted by pregnant women will bear abundantly, while a tree planted by an old man will bear little and die young. Conversely, Choctaw legend prohibits planting by menstruating women.

❧

Fruits and vegetables with shapes similar to human body parts have been thought to take on some of the attributes of the organ. The English found both sweet potatoes and white potatoes erotic. The sweet potato was regarded by Elizabethans as a powerful aphrodisiac, looking something like the male organ, they thought. When the white potato reached England it assumed some of its cousin's reputation and came to represent testicles. When Falstaff declares, in Shakespeare's *Henry IV*, "Let the sky rain potatoes," he had sweet potatoes in mind, and may not have been referring just to vegetables.

❧

The best cucumber crops are believed to come from seeds planted by vigorous young men. Old men's cucumber crops are small and sparse.

ATTRACTING BIRDS

DRAWING HUMMINGBIRDS

T o attract hummingbirds, plant flowers with tubular blossoms, preferably red ones. Some very effective hummingbird attractors are trumpet vine (*Campsis* spp.), columbine (*Aquilegia* spp.), clarkia (*Clarkia* spp.), montbretia (*Crocosmia crocosmiflora*), honeysuckle (*Lonicera* spp.), fuchsia (*Fuchsia* spp.), buddleia (*Buddleia* spp.)—also a good butterfly attractor—bearberry (*Arctostaphylos uva-ursi*), flowering quince (*Chaenomeles* spp.), and some veronicas. If you live where it will grow, one of the best is California fuchsia (*Zauschneria* spp.).

One technique that works beautifully is a hummingbird feeder. You don't need special food, just a solution made up of one part regular refined sugar to four parts water. Don't use food coloring in the sugar water—instead choose a bright red feeder with feeding ports designed like flowers. Clean the feeder often and never use honey in the solution, as it can cause a fatal fungal disease.

If you want hummers to stay, include ferns in your garden; having large trees in your yard or your neighborhood is also a bonus. Ferns are a source of nesting material for hummingbirds, who will seek a safe place such as a solid shade tree for a nesting site. Lichens are also valuable nesting material. And if you see spiderwebs in your garden, leave them alone—the hummingbirds will collect silk from the webs for their tiny nests.

ATTRACTING SONGBIRDS

Many birds are seed and berry eaters, so make sure to include plants that bear these in your garden. Consider wild strawberries, cherries, blackberries, elderberries, viburnums, sumacs, cotoneasters, hollies, and pyracantha for the fruits. A selection of sunflowers, millets, zinnias, coreopsis, cosmos, and amaranths should provide a banquet of seeds.

❦

Have water available for birds if you want to see more of them in your garden. You don't need a fancy birdbath—any simple shallow container is perfect for birds. Use a large clay saucer, the kind that is meant to sit beneath garden pots. And it's important to keep the birdbath fresh, clean, and algae-free.

❦

I put out birdseed in the winter, but have found that as spring takes hold, the birds seem to lose their taste for store-bought seed. When it's obvious the birds aren't eating the offered birdseed, or are picking out only the sunflower seeds, I stop putting it out until cold weather arrives again.

❦

Some birds will be attracted if you put up birdhouses, although this isn't a surefire method. Certain birds demand a particular style of architecture—purple martins, for example, like dormitory-style housing placed well off the ground. We have a pair of bluebirds that returns every year to a small cottage placed about 5 feet (1.5m) above the ground on a power pole. Woodpeckers and sapsuckers usually choose a hollowed-out area in a high dead tree. Note that some ornamental birdhouses make nice garden accents but may actually be unsafe for birds—check that the birdhouse you buy is intended for use if you want to bring birds to your garden.

Controlling Insects

nsects don't have to be a problem, especially in the home garden. Nature has done a good job of arranging itself so that animals, insects, and plants are kept in balance, and no insect gets to be so numerous that it becomes a pest.

If you have a few aphids, they aren't going to do much damage but will provide food for ladybugs, which will then hang out in your garden and keep matters under control.

Problems arise when something swings out of balance (a situation often caused by the gardener), and sometimes the remedies applied actually make things worse. I find the best controls are mechanical rather than chemical—floating row covers are a good example. Biological controls, such as introducing ladybugs or tiny parasitic wasps, are also good choices, since they will take care of the problem without changing the basic ecology of the garden. Following are some ideas for keeping your garden clear of devastating insect pests.

Remember that all insecticides, whether they are derived from natural plant parts or created by a chemist's art, are designed to kill. They should always be handled with respect and used sparingly; labels should be read completely and their warnings taken seriously.

GENERAL INSECT CONTROLS

Including a variety of plants and mixing your plantings means that your garden will be much more resistant to insect predation than a monoculture would be. Grouping all your broccoli together makes it convenient for the cabbage looper to find and decimate your broccoli plants. Some order is necessary, of course, for reasons of convenience and management, but a varied garden is a healthier one. It's the corn-bean-squash effect writ large.

BT

Bacillus thuringiensis (Bt), a caterpillar killer, is widely used as an organic pesticide, and is promoted as safe for humans and harmless to the environment. This is true, with a huge caveat—Bt kills *all* caterpillars, not just ones that grow up to be cabbage loopers or tomato hornworms. So if you spray Bt indiscriminately, be aware that you'll wipe out all the butterflies in your garden. For home gardeners, cabbage worms and cabbage loopers are rarely a severe problem, and can be handpicked and destroyed easily. Tomato hornworms are huge, and can easily be plucked off tomato plants.

There are special strains of Bt formulated specifically for mosquito larva or for certain beetles. If you need to use Bt, spray it sparingly, use it when the air is still, and limit your treatment to the affected plant.

MILKY SPORE DISEASE

Milky spore disease is the common name for the bacteria *Bacillus popilliae*. It is used to control insects, particularly Japanese beetle grubs and larvae that live in the soil. Like all pest controls, it should be applied carefully and according to package directions.

ROTENONE

Rotenone is one of the insecticides classified as "botanical," that is, derived from a plant. It has been in use for a long time, with the first recorded use in the middle of the nineteenth century. It is derived from South American plants of the genus *Lonchocarpus*. Rotenone is generally used in a dust-like form that is obtained by grinding up the desiccated plant root.

Rotenone is used against a wide variety of sucking and leaf-eating insects, such as beetles and caterpillars, including the Colorado potato beetle and the cabbageworm. Rotenone is the most toxic of the botanical insecticides, and should be used with caution. Because it kills bees and other pollinators as well as pests, apply in the evening after bees have returned to their hives. It is especially toxic to fish, so should never be used where runoff can enter streams or lakes.

SABADILLA

Sabadilla has become popular in recent years, as it is low in toxicity to mammals. It is derived from the ground seeds of a tropical plant, *Schoenocaulon officinale*. The dust can be very irritating to some people, however, so a dust mask should be worn while applying it. Sabadilla acts as a stomach and contact poison for various bugs, including the squash bug, stink bug, and harlequin bug. It has also proven its worth against leaf-feeding caterpillars and thrips.

PYRETHRUM

As you might suspect, pyrethrum comes from the pyrethrum daisy (*Chrysanthemum cinerariifolium*). Pyrethrum is often combined with rotenone in dusts and sprays. Together, they quickly kill flying insects that are sprayed or dusted directly. However, pyrethrum does not persist, but rapidly degrades in sunlight and dampness, making it environmentally friendly. It is also approved for use in food preparation areas, since it has low toxicity to humans.

RYANIA

Ryania comes from a South American shrub of the same name, and is used in the form of a powdered extract of roots and stems. The powder is mixed with water to make a spray. It is useful against coddling moths (a serious pest of apples), caterpillars, leaf-eating beetles, and thrips. It is relatively nontoxic to mammals, and persists on leaves longer than most other botanicals, making it useful as a residual killer.

NEEM

Neem is extracted from the seeds of the neem tree of India. Neem has long been used in pharmaceuticals in India, even in toothpaste. As you might expect, it is very safe for humans' use. However, it deters feeding of leaf-chewing beetles and caterpillars, and seems to have an effect on insect hormones, causing them to die as they molt. Because of its safety record, it has been approved by the Environmental Protection Agency for use on any plant, edible or ornamental.

HORTICULTURAL OILS AND INSECTICIDAL SOAPS

Both of these products make their contribution by killing insects as you spray them. They do not have a residual toxic effect, either for insects or humans. Horticultural oils, derived from petroleum, kill mostly by suffocating or smothering insects. Horticultural oils have been much improved recently, and now can be used for a wide variety of plants. At one time their use was confined to trees in a dormant state, especially fruit trees. Check the label for precautions.

Insecticidal soaps were all the rage a few years ago, but proved to have limited value. They are perfectly safe, work on contact, and quickly dry to a harmless coating. Insecticidal soaps are quite effective for small insects, and even for Japanese beetles, if you can manage to spray the solution directly on the bug. The problem is that you must hit the insect directly and the soap has no residual effect, that is, it won't continue to work after that first spray. Some plants are sensitive to these soaps, so be sure to read the package cautions.

LADYBUGS

When you use an insect to control the population of another insect, you are employing "biological" controls. Most people are familiar with ladybugs, or lady beetles, and their appetite for aphids. Ladybugs will also eat other soft-bodied insects. When you buy them, either from a garden center or by mail, you will get a container filled with a specified number of adult ladybugs. They will be thirsty, so open the container and scatter a little water over them. The container can be kept in the refrigerator until conditions are right to release them. The best time to let the ladybugs go is during the evening. If it has not rained, water your garden first, taking care to wet foliage.

A common complaint about buying and releasing ladybugs is their tendency to leave home and search out greener pastures. Reconcile yourself to the idea that many will fly elsewhere. But if you have things for them to eat—aphids or the nectar of blooming plants—enough will stick around to lay eggs. The larva are excellent aphid hunters. If you have a healthy garden, a resident population of ladybugs will establish itself, and will keep insect populations in check.

LACEWINGS

Lacewings are purchased in the egg stage. As the little lacewings hatch, they make a dash for food, preferring thrips, small caterpillars, mites, moth eggs, and mealybugs. They also control aphids. The recommended "dose" is two lacewing eggs per square foot of garden space.

GREENHOUSE PREDATORS

There are various insect predators available for use in greenhouses, including tiny wasps (which don't sting humans), predatory mites, and a lady beetle that is a specific remedy for mealybugs.

Praying Mantises

I'd avoid the praying mantis. It was once a popular choice as a biological control, but further study has shown that it is an alarmingly effective predator, eating everything, both good and bad (including its own young). If you see one or two in your garden, you'll find them interesting to watch, but it really isn't necessary to purchase a herd of them.

Beneficial Nematodes

One of the persistent problems gardeners encounter is nematodes, tiny worms that can destroy plant roots. However, there are also beneficial nematodes, which will parasitize some nasty fellows, such as cutworms, white grubs, root weevils, and other nematodes. You buy beneficial nematodes by the millions, but they are so small that millions fit into a small container. The nematodes are mixed with water and sprinkled on wet soil, where they will immediately enter and search out dinner. Dry air and sunlight will kill them, so they should be applied in the evening, ideally when there are calm breezes.

A Gallery of Insect Pests

Aphids

 phids are prevalent garden pests but people worry about them too much, I think. It's easy enough to rub them out, literally. Or you can hose them off with a strong spray. They come in several colors, by the way, including green, pink, red, and black.

Ladybugs love aphids, and even some small birds will eat them.

Budworms

The geranium budworm and tobacco budworm, close relatives, are serious pests in California and in some of the neighboring mountain and mild-winter areas. The adult moth lays an egg on each geranium bud. The worm hatches, eats through the bud, ruining it, and then moves on to the rest of the plant. Bt works, sprayed locally on the geranium (or the rose or petunia, which are alternate hosts).

COLORADO POTATO BEETLES

Colorado potato beetles are black-striped beetles that begin with small, yellow egg clusters. Despite its name, this beetle is a problem mostly on the East Coast and in the Midwest.

Hand-picking is most effective for a mild infestation, which is usually all that affects home gardens.

There is a specific Bt, called Bt var. san diego, for this pest, but it is effective only on the larva, as is true for all Bts. Rotenone, neem, and pyrethrum sprays are also effective organic controls.

CORN EARWORMS AND CORN BORERS

The corn earworm is a close relative of the geranium budworm (the whole family is disreputable). Earworms can be prevented by putting mineral oil on the corn silks after they wither but before they turn brown. Timing is critical. Or you might just accept the possibility you will get some of these worms and simply cut off the bad tip of the ear and eat the rest.

Corn borers are quite a different matter from corn earworms. They are found mostly in the East and Midwest, but can attack everywhere except Florida and the West Coast. Adult moths lay their eggs on the underside of new corn leaves. The hatched larvae begin chewing into the plant right away, eventually going into the ear; if you see bent or broken corn tassels, you probably have borers. In bad infestations, multiple borers will be found in a single ear. Favorable weather—wet springs and dry summers—inhibit borers somewhat.

You can reduce the number of borers by avoiding very early or very late plantings, which bypass the peak borer periods. Hand-picking the insects is a chore, but cutting open the stalks that have borer holes may expose borers, and you can tease them out.

❧

A directed application of Bt in leaf whorls on cornstalks will kill the borers. Once they actually get into the stalks or ears, it's too late for the Bt to have an effect.

❧

Parasitic flies and wasps prey on borer larvae, as do ladybugs, so import some of these into your garden.

❧

If you have had borers, destroy the cornstalks after harvest to prevent the borers from overwintering.

CUCUMBER BEETLES

Cucumber beetles, both spotted and striped varieties, are nasty customers. They look a lot like beneficial ladybugs except for their green color and their criminal disposition.

❧

Sanitation is a good preventative—cleaning up potential overwintering sites in dead vines and other plant material is likely to avert outbreaks of this beetle.

❧

Planting early may outwit cucumber beetles, as the plants will grow beyond the seedling stage before the cucumber beetles are born—the beetles feed on the seedlings rather than mature plants. On the other hand, cucumbers and other cucurbits such as pumpkins and squash are prime targets, but can't be planted before the weather warms both air and soil so timing is important. Plant after the danger of frost has passed and warm the soil quickly by covering it with clear or black plastic.

CUTWORMS

Cutworms, moth larvae that rest in tight circles just beneath the soil during the day, emerge at night and will eat through tender stems of just-set-out plants. Prevent this by putting a stiff collar around the plant stem, allowing about half an inch to an inch (1–2.5cm) of clearance. Any kind of fairly rigid paper or cardboard works well. The collar should be pushed an inch or two (2.5–5cm) into the ground and should extend two or three inches (5–7cm) above ground level.

Cutworms can also cause lots of damage to lawns. Flooding the affected area (a brown island in a green lawn) with water to which some dish-washing soap has been added will bring the cutworms to the surface, where they can be picked off.

EARWIGS

Earwigs eat plant leaves; they seem to prefer dead leaves, and can do quite a respectable job of eating aphids and cleaning up debris. But if there aren't any dead leaves, earwigs will move on to green leaves, and can be devastating to seedlings.

There are no really effective poisons for earwigs. Diatomaceous earth is sometimes recommended, and can be effective as a barrier to keep earwigs out of a particular area, but it's not a very efficient way of pre-venting earwig infestations throughout a garden or lawn. Earwigs feed at night, and if you see a few during the day you probably have many times more. The best way to control them is to tidy up your garden, digging in any dead plant material lying around and removing unused pots, which deprives earwigs of their daytime hiding places.

Since earwigs like to hide during the day, trick them. At night, put out narrow tubes of rolled newspaper. The earwigs are attracted not to the paper itself but to the safe haven provided by the tubes. In the morning the tubes of paper will hold sleeping earwigs. You can gently shake the bugs into a dish of soapy water, where they will drown.

❧

Shallow saucers filled with vegetable oil will attract earwigs, but you'll end up with saucers full of oiled carcasses. If you don't find the disposal too distasteful, this is a good method.

FIREANTS

While fireants won't harm your plants, they will attack humans and animals; the stings are very painful, and may even be deadly if you are allergic.

❧

A mixture of manure tea and blackstrap molasses has proven effective in many cases. Make some manure tea by steeping a cheesecloth bag full of steer or cow manure in a bucket of water for one week. This will become very "fragrant." To that solution add two or three ounces of blackstrap molasses and pour it on the fireant mound to kill the ants.

❧

Another procedure reputed to be effective involves uncooked instant grits. Scatter the grits (these must be uncooked and must be the instant form) over the fireant hill. The ants will eat it and die. They may even get some back to the queen, who will then also die. While not scientifically proven, this remedy has reportedly worked for many people.

FLEA BEETLES

Flea beetles can be a serious problem for seedlings, although they will eat the leaves of a range of plants. A parasitic nematode will handle flea beetles at the grub stage, while floating row covers will keep out adults.

❧

Flea beetles are attracted to white, and will jump on a piece of white paper placed on the ground. One control for whitefly, which is attracted to yellow, is to coat a yellow card with a thin film of motor oil, and put it out where the whiteflies will see it, jump on it, and be trapped. If I had flea beetles, I think I'd try something similar with a white card and some sticky transparent stuff, perhaps mineral oil.

JAPANESE BEETLES

Japanese beetles are vicious plant predators and can quickly reduce a plant to skeletonized shreds. They attack most vegetables and are a special menace to roses. Their grubs can ruin lawns.

Milky spore, a strain of bacteria called *Bacillus popilliae*, is effective against the grubs, reducing next year's population though not doing much for the adults you already have.

Floating row covers keep adult beetles off vegetables and flowers.

Beetle traps are available. Some say traps just attract more beetles to your yard, but if the insects are indeed being trapped, well, that's the point.

Insecticidal soaps, rotenone, and pyrethrum are effective controls, but you need to apply often and be vigilant.

PILL BUGS AND SOW BUGS

Sowbugs and pill bugs are very similar, but the pill bug is black and rolls itself up into a tight ball when disturbed while the sowbug is gray and kind of folds up rather than making a tight ball. These bugs are active in the spring, and generally will eat decayed plant material, cleaning up some for you. If there is not enough of their preferred food available they will turn to living plants, especially seedlings, and will also feed on melons or tomatoes that have broken skin. The best approach to ridding your garden of pill bugs is good cleanup—keep the ground clear of dead plants, which attract them, and things they can hide under during the day. An interesting note—pill bugs aren't bugs at all, but rather crustaceans, related to lobsters and shrimp, and breathe through gills. Their proper name, rarely used, is wood louse.

ROSE CHAFERS AND ROOT WEEVILS

Controls for rose chafers and root weevils are similar. There are nematodes available to attack and destroy them in their larval-grub stage, while floating row covers will keep the adults away from your plants.

🌿

Rotenone, sprayed at dusk for root weevils and at any time of day for rose chafers, works well on adults.

🌿

Cultivate the soil around affected plants often to uncover the grubs of root weevils and rose chafers. This will expose them to hungry birds, who will be glad to help take care of your problem.

SCALE INSECTS

Scale insects, of which there are several different types, are really odd. Adults live their entire lives in the same place, usually on a plant leaf or stem, encased in a waxy shell. They suck juices from the plant. Scale insects' eggs hatch beneath the adults' shells, and then venture out to find their own feeding sites. Scale insects are primarily a problem with citrus and olive trees, and with indoor plants.

🌿

When an infestation of scale insects is light, you'll be able to scrape or peel the little lumps off with your fingernail.

Scale is hunted by several natural predators and parasites, including parasitic wasps and certain types of lady beetles (*Chilococorus nigritis*).

An old home remedy for getting rid of scale insects is to wipe them off with the tip of a cloth soaked in buttermilk; the buttermilk softens the wax and makes it easier to remove the insect beneath. You can also use rubbing alcohol in the same fashion.

Horticultural oil can be effective in controlling scale.

SNAILS AND SLUGS

For many gardeners the arrival of spring is darkened by the emergence of hungry snails and slugs. Snails can denude a shrub overnight. You may think those lettuce seeds you bought were old or defective, since you did everything right, planted them two weeks ago, and haven't seen any seedlings yet. Perhaps you haven't spotted any seedlings but the slugs almost certainly have, and are polishing them off every night, just as the tiny leaflets emerge. Following are several ways to control snails and slugs. (Slugs, by the way, are just naked snails, gastropods without shells.)

Barriers work best to protect individual shrubs and larger plants—the idea here is to surround your plants with something slugs and snails won't cross. Diatomaceous earth, a powdery substance made of the crushed skeletons of ancient sea creatures, abrades the undersides of the snail, so generally snails won't attempt to cross a barrier made of it.

Copper strips set up around your plants interact with the snail/slug secretions, giving the insects a slight electrical charge and causing them to move away. Copper is expensive but pennies, especially shiny new ones, work just as well and are eminently recyclable.

You can also trap slugs and snails. They are attracted to the sugar and yeast in beer, so if you have stale beer, or can get some from a neighbor, place a saucer in the ground with the edge at ground level or slightly above. Slugs and snails will slither in and drown. Note that the traps must be emptied and refilled daily. Be aware, too, that many dogs have a "beer tooth," and may deplete your bait if they're allowed near it.

One easy and inexpensive way to trap snails and slugs is to make your own trap out of an empty plastic bottle, like those that hold soda or water.

This is easily done by cutting off the top portion of the bottle and inverting it over the bottom portion so that the bottle neck now faces down toward the bottom of the bottle. Staple the bottle pieces together with the two pieces in position. Put some commercial slug bait in the bottom of the bottle and lay the bottle on its side in the garden. Slugs will find their way in easily enough but will usually be unable to crawl out. The beauty of this simple method is that small children, dogs, and other animals will not be able to get at the bait.

One of the most effective snail preventatives is harvesting and disposing. Go out a little after dark—around 10 o'clock or so—with a flashlight and search your plants and the ground around them. If you have snails, they will all be feasting at this hour, and can be picked up and put in a bag, tied off with a twist tie, and set out with the garbage. Damp soil around your plants will draw out an amazing number of snails after dark.

❧

Another way to trap snails and slugs is with a wooden board placed on damp ground. The insects will hide under the board and can then be captured and dispatched in the morning. One reasonably aesthetic method of disposal is to drop the slugs and snails into a container of salted water, or you can simply put them in a plastic bag, tie it off, and set it out with the trash.

SQUASH BUGS

Squash bugs, sometimes called stink bugs, mainly affect pumpkins and winter squash. The eggs appear as a hard brown mass on the underside of leaves in spring; destroy these eggs if you find them. It's easiest to simply pull off the leaf and put it in the trash.

❧

Squash bugs are similar to earwigs in that they are nocturnal, so they can be trapped under flat boards and crushed. When you do that, you'll find out how they got their nickname.

DEALING WITH DEER

little research turns up dozens of ways of deer-proofing the garden—each of them worked for someone at some time, but the very volume of remedies means that none of them worked for everyone all the time.

DEER-PROOF PLANTS

Hungry deer will eat almost any plant, so lists of "deer-proof" plants are far from infallible. Still, planting deer's least favorite menu may send them on to a site with tastier plants. Trees that deer avoid include cedar, cypress, ash, magnolia, olive, spruce, pine, and oak. Among the shrubs are abelia, barberry, buddleia, cotoneaster, daphne, juniper, nandina, myrtle, oleander (highly poisonous—deer aren't dumb), potentilla, pyracantha, lilac, and viburnum. Plumbago, columbine, campanula, iris, monarda, gloriosa daisy, poppies, clarkia, and pincushion flower may also be overlooked by browsing deer. Just remember that when times are tough a deer will eat anything available to survive, just as a human would.

One popular approach for repelling deer has been to hang slivers of Irish Spring soap around the garden, but the deer in my area seemed attracted by the perfume.

The following homemade repellent may prove effective for short periods of time: Blend together one egg, two ounces of Chinese chili oil (carried in the gourmet or international food section of supermarkets or available in Chinese markets anywhere), and water to fill two-thirds of a blender container. To this concoction add a dissolved bouillon cube, mix well, and strain. Add enough water to make one gallon, and spray the mixture on those plants you want to protect.

BARRIERS

I have been successful in protecting specific plants or plantings with woven garden fabric, available at garden centers and through catalogs. But remember that the cloth protects only what it covers, and it's probably not possible to cover everything. Reserve the fabric for your valuable plants.

❦

There is one guaranteed deer solution—an 8-foot (2.4m) fence made out of strong wire. Farm supply stores will know it as hog wire or pasture wire. Flimsy chicken wire won't do the job, as deer simply knock it down. Special deer fences made of green plastic mesh, designed to fade into the landscape, are also available. Installed to a height of ten feet (3m), they are quite effective.

❦

A variation on the deer fence solution is to run three wires, at 7, 5, and 3 feet (1.65, 1.5, and 1m), on posts canted outwards, with the top wire the furthest away from the area you are protecting. Deer can jump high, and they can jump a considerable distance, but they can't do both in the same jump. The slant and the height of the wires will look dangerous to the deer and they will search for an easier spot to conquer.

❦

Another effective method is an electrified fence. These can get expensive and elaborate; you won't want to make the protection more expensive than the protected. A single electrified wire, which is usually sufficient to contain cattle or horses, simply makes an interesting hurdle for deer. An effective design uses seven wires fastened to 7-foot (1.65m) -long timbers supported by 4-foot (1.2m) posts so the timber makes a 45-degree angle with the ground. This type of barrier is not only difficult to install, it requires constant trimming to ensure that vegetation will not grow up and short out the wires or drain the current into the ground. A farm supply outlet is the best place to obtain electric fence information and supplies, including chargers and insulators.

BIRD DETERRENTS

Birds are delightful additions to the garden, but can pose big problems as marauders of ripe fruit. One friend says he knows his cherries are ripe when the birds start to eat them. Many methods have been tried to scare birds away.

Scarecrows don't frighten finches much less crows—instead, try large balloons with "eyes" printed on them. There are also a variety of faux predators—including inflatable owls and hawks and rubber snakes—that will keep fruit thieves away, at least for a short while.

One effective way to keep birds away from fruit is to cover the tree or bush with fine netting—it is something of a hassle to install, but will ensure that you get a fruit harvest for yourself.

Here's a homemade solution found effective by some gardeners—put a hole through an aluminum pie plate and tie it to the fruit tree. The fluttering of the shiny reflective surface tends to make birds wary and keeps them away from your tree.

Make sure to install netting or other deterrents such as predator models or pie plates just as fruit begins to ripen. If you prepare too early, the birds may discover ways around barriers or stop being fooled by fake predators. If you prepare too late, the birds may be willing to take more risks to get at the fruit they know from experience is ripe and delicious.

Some gardeners swear by another simple bird repellent: cut some onion rings and hang them individually from branches of the tree. Apparently, birds hate the smell and will leave the fruit alone. Certainly inexpensive and positively organic, this method is definitely worth a try.

Handling Other Animal Pests

Rabbits

R abbits can be a nuisance in the garden, grazing on a wide variety of plants. There are several approaches to minimizing their damage. I say minimizing, because if you have rabbits in your vicinity you will have them in your garden unless the space is completely fenced. But take comfort, as rabbits aren't usually so much of a problem that they warrant extensive, expensive action.

To protect valuable trees from rabbit attacks on bark and trunks, wrap the trunks with poultry wire to a height of two feet (60cm) or so, with the wire extending a couple of inches (5cm) into the soil.

Rabbits are repelled by some scents. They don't much like onions or garlic, and scattering some of these plants throughout your garden can keep rabbits at a distance. Dried blood (blood meal) is also an effective repellent, but carnivores—dogs and cats especially—will be attracted by the scent.

Other deterrents that you might try include pepper, both black and cayenne. Sprinkle it about the garden or mix it with water and spray it on your plants. A plant reputed to repel rabbits is dusty miller (*Senecio cinerara*), and it's certainly worth a try if you are plagued by these furry critters.

An animal-lovers' solution to dealing with rabbits is to plant especially for them, surrounding your garden with things they like, so they will eat those instead of your more valuable plantings. Try an edging of soybeans or lettuce around the perimeter of your garden.

Gophers

Gophers have plagued me for years. I'm an expert on these animals, but not on their eradication. Gophers are a difficult pest particularly in regions west of the Mississippi, and they are well adapted to the West Coast. They have natural predators—owls and gopher snakes—but the owls are becoming scarce and it's just the luck of the draw whether you happen to have a resident gopher snake.

Gophers are vegetarians, and seem to prefer the most expensive and ornamental of plants. They consider tulip bulbs a special treat.

Poisons aren't usually very effective when used against gophers, and you run the danger of a poisoned gopher becoming dinner for an unsuspecting predator. Some gardeners will run water down the gopher holes, but the subterranean passageways are so extensive that this technique is not very practical and can waste huge amounts of water.

"Humane" traps work best—these are traps that kill gophers instantly. (While you may be able to find traps that capture gophers alive, you are then faced with the dilemma of what to do with them. Releasing them elsewhere means that you are likely setting them free to feast in somebody else's backyard buffet.) Trapping technique is important. Starting at the visible surface hole that first alerted you to the presence of gophers, dig down and locate the main horizontal highway. Place two traps there, one on either side of the main road. Attach a chain or rope to the traps, and fasten the other end of the rope to a stake or a tree on the surface to prevent the gopher from dragging the trap deep into his burrow.

Plug the hole you have made with fresh greens like grass or vegetable tops, anything fairly soft and fragrant, to attract the gopher(s). Then cover the hole so that no light can get through. You'll have to check the traps frequently. The gopher may pile fresh dirt into the trap. Clear this and keep waiting. Be patient—gophers are clever, and it may take a while to catch them.

Some animal-loving gardeners report sucess in keeping gophers out of the garden with a perimeter planting of spurge (*Euphobia lathyrus*). This plant repels the furry pest, but must completely surround the garden to be an effective deterrent.

MOLES

Moles are carnivores, and eat worms, insects, and larva. You find them most often in good, well-tended soil that has a substantial population of grubs and earthworms. Moles rarely eat plants, but their tunnels can expose plant roots to drying air. They are mainly an aesthetic problem for the gardener, as their tunnels and dirt piles disfigure lawns and gardens.

Trapping is the best way to get rid of moles. A spring trap set into the mole run from above is the most effective, but kills the animal. A patient cat with a killer instinct will also help you eradicate moles. If you find these methods distasteful, you might learn to live with the mole tunnels. Alternatively, you could try eliminating the grubs they feed upon from your soil using milky spore disease.

FIGHTING PLANT DISEASES

BLACK SPOT

lack spot is a serious disease of roses, and is particularly problematic in the Northeast and on the Pacific coast. A mild case results in circular spots, black in the center and often with a yellow outer ring. A severe case will cause all the leaves to drop, leaving a weakened plant.

Eliminating the conditions that lead to black spot is the best way to protect your roses. The fungus spores that cause black spot overwinter on old leaves and damaged canes. Clean up all old leaves under your roses before winter sets in and prune off any damaged canes. Black spot-resistant roses do exist, and if you live in a prime black spot area you should plant only those cultivars. Your local nursery or a specialty grower will be happy to guide you in selecting a disease-resistant rose.

There is a home remedy you can try to combat black spot: apply a mixture of baking soda and either dishwashing detergent or summer oil (a horticultural oil used as a base for a variety of fungus and insect conditions). To make black spot spray, mix two teaspoons of baking soda and the two tablespoons of summer oil in a gallon of water; or use one tablespoon each of baking soda and dish soap in a gallon of water. Spray away, beginning in the spring and continuing weekly. It's best to spray early in the morning, so the leaves dry during the day.

FIREBLIGHT

Fireblight is a serious disease of apple, crabapple, pear, and quince trees, as well as hawthorns and mountain ash. Shrubs affected include cotoneasters and pyracantha. Notice a connection there? All these plants are relatives of the rose. Fireblight is a bacterial disease, and strikes suddenly and hard, killing flowering shoots quickly. If you see a branch that looks burned, it is usually afflicted with fireblight. This disease usually attacks in early spring, when the bacteria are spread to opened blossoms by rainfall. Bees spread the disease further as they pollinate, and the infection, if not stopped, can make its way into the main trunk of the tree or shrub quickly.

The best fireblight control for home gardeners is to prune out and burn affected branches as soon as they're sighted. Cut well below the area that appears to be affected. Disinfect your pruners or saw with undiluted bleach after *each and every* cut. Tender new growth is most at risk, so if you have seen fireblight in your area make sure you don't overfertilize, especially with nitrogen, which encourages vigorous leafy growth.

If you have consistent problems with fireblight, you have a couple of choices. There are some resistant varieties; consult your local nursery for a list of suggested plants suitable to your area. Alternatively, you could stop growing the plants that are susceptible.

MILDEW

Powdery mildew and downy mildew are similar, and sometimes confused. Powdery mildew starts out as small white patches and can rapidly spread to cover entire leaves. It's a special problem for squash and squash relatives, but will also attack lots of other plants, including roses, chrysanthemums, and dahlias. Powdery mildew can spread in dry conditions (unlike most mildews, which only spread in the presence of moisture). It is the biggest problem in areas with little or no summer rain.

Downy mildew is found on the undersides of leaves, spreads rapidly on wet leaves, and is more common in areas of substantial summer rain and in areas with cool summers. It is a real problem with cucumbers and grapes, and, like the powdery stuff, can attack a wide variety of plants. Control of either mildew is difficult.

🌿

Since powdery mildew likes dry conditions, overhead watering can deter it. The baking soda–detergent spray recommended for black spot may also help (see Black Spot on page 65).

🌿

Downy mildew is best controlled by irrigating plants at soil level or below so that leaves stay dry. Water early in the morning so if leaves do get wet they will dry quickly.

🌿

Keep the areas around plants clean of fallen leaves or other plant parts to prevent reinfestation.

RUST

Rust is a group of fungal diseases. Usually thought of as a rose problem (and it is indeed a problem for roses), different strains of rust affect a wide variety of plants.

Each strain of rust has evolved to infect a specific type of plant; rose rust, for example, will not infect snapdragons. There are rust-resistant varieties of many plants, so if rust is a problem in your garden, look for those varieties.

❦

All forms of rust need water to spawn and spread, so keeping leaves dry is an important method of control. Water your plants at the base.

❦

Some fungicides have been proven effective against rust, especially on roses, so check your garden center for a product suited to the type of plant infected.

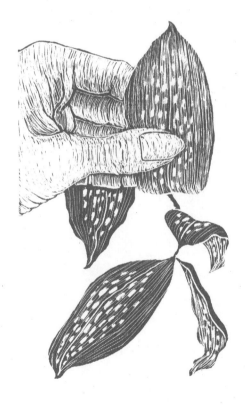

VIRUSES

Viral diseases are much more of a problem in commercial agriculture than they are in the home garden. Viruses usually don't kill their host plants, but disfigure or distort them. Rose mosaic virus, for example, can result in yellowed or blotched leaves or in a general lack of vigor. Viruses are spread by insects, especially aphids, and by man. Thrips can also carry viruses, as can other insects. Tobacco mosaic virus, which will attack tomato plants, is spread by humans who handle tobacco and then handle plants. Tobacco and tomato plants are both in the nightshade family, as are potatoes.

But humans can spread all sorts of viruses, and they don't have to be smokers to do it.

There is no cure for viral diseases, either human or plant. You can reduce the chances of your plants contracting viruses by controlling the insects, especially aphids, that transmit plant viruses.

PLANT HARDINESS ZONES

he seasons of the year arrive at different times, depending on where you live. Latitude plays an important part in the parade of seasons, of course, as does altitude. The United States Department of Agriculture (USDA) has designed a map that organizes regions into various "hardiness zones," offering a rough guide to determining the best plants suitable for your climate. But the zone map considers only one variable—average annual low temperatures. The problem becomes clear when the weather deviates from the average: for example, a particular location may have an exceptionally cold winter, with temperatures 10 degrees or more below the average, and the garden will typically suffer.

Nor does the hardiness zone map consider climactic differentials. I live in the Siskiyou mountains of Oregon, which is 1,400 feet above sea level. We have a typical Mediterranean climate, with rain from mid-October to mid-April and little precipitation at other times of the year—the zone map places us in Zone 8. The Gulf Coast of the Florida panhandle, Alabama, and Mississippi are also in Zone 8, though they have a far different climate and a far different list of plants that will do well.

❧

You can purchase a poster-sized hardiness zone map from a gardening catalog or through the USDA. The chart below will help you determine the zone in which you live, or you can simply call your local extension agent, ask the folks at a nearby garden center, or find out from a knowledgeable gardener in your neighborhood.

RANGE OF AVERAGE ANNUAL MINIMUM TEMPERATURES FOR EACH ZONE		
	Fahrenheit (°F)	Celsius (°C)
Zone 1	Below −50°	Below −45.6°
Zone 2	−50° to −40°	−45.6° to −40°
Zone 3	−40° to −30°	−40° to −34.4°
Zone 4	−30° to −20°	−34.4° to −28.9°
Zone 5	−20° to −10°	−28.9° to −23.3°
Zone 6	−10° to 0°	−23.3° to −17.8°
Zone 7	0° to 10°	−17.8° to −12.2°
Zone 8	10° to 20°	−12.2° to −6.7°
Zone 9	20° to 30°	−6.7° to −1.1°
Zone 10	30° to 40°	−1.1° to 4.4°
Zone 11	Above 40°	Above 4.4°

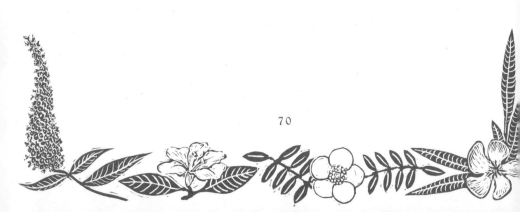

Weather Problems

ou have done all the right things—pulled the weeds, prepared the soil, gotten the garden ready for the first planting. And the weather turns cold and wet. Well, you think, this isn't going to last forever and, full of hope, you set out the tomato and pepper plants. And nothing happens. A week later, the plants look just the same as they did when you put them in the ground. Two weeks later, no change, no growth, nothing. Will there ever be a harvest? Why aren't the plants growing? Maybe I should add some fertilizer, you think. Not so quick.

In all likelihood, what's wrong is that the soil is too cold. The plants are living, and probably slowly, very slowly, making new roots. But until the weather warms up, your tomatoes and peppers and melons and whatever else you thought would get an early start will just sit there, seemingly unchanged. Fertilizer added now will have one of two effects. It might not do anything at all, and that's the good thing. The bad thing is that it might kill your tomatoes, peppers, or other plants, burning their delicate roots.

Eventually, just as surely as day follows night, the sun will come out, the soil will warm up, and your plants will take off in a frenzy of growth. So if it's a cold, wet, late spring, be patient. Mother Nature is running things, and she will let the plants know when it's time. And later you'll notice an odd thing. The date you harvest your first ripe tomato will be just about the same date you harvested the first tomato last year.

WEATHER LORE

eople who spend a lot of time outdoors soon begin to notice weather patterns, and they develop a knack for figuring out what weather is approaching. There are signs all around, if you know where to look.

FOLK BELIEFS

The familiar saying "red sky at night, sailor's delight, red sky in the morning, sailors take warning" is based on science, not superstition. Weather most often comes from the west. If the sky is clear for a long way west, the air tends to have a lot of dust and smoke in it, leading to a red sunset, since the red rather than blue light is transmitted better in hazy conditions. Thus, red sunset will be followed by clear weather. A red sky in the morning, on the other hand, can be caused by low clouds, which carry with them the possibility of bad weather.

❧

One common country observation says that if, while it's raining, chimney smoke hangs close to the ground it will continue to rain for a while. If the smoke rises straight up, clear weather is approaching.

❧

If rain doesn't begin until after seven in the morning, it will rain all day, and maybe for more than a day. But a foggy morning usually means a clear afternoon.

ANIMAL AND INSECT PREDICTORS

According to tradition, migrating birds will fly high in good weather, but low to the ground if a storm is approaching.

❧

Bees are said to cease their activity if a storm is imminent, but the weather will be good for a while if ants and spiders are very active.

❧

I have my own method of learning when it's going to rain: my cats will come into the house and go to sleep during the day, or will stay in at night. Never fails.

Crickets can tell the temperature, and they announce it regularly. Count the number of cricket chirps in 14 seconds, add 40, and you will have a very accurate estimate of the temperature in degrees Fahrenheit.

Some people say that cows will face east if the weather is going to be good, west if it's going to storm. That's backwards to me, since cows always stand with their tails toward a storm, and most weather comes from the west. Others believe that cows lie down when it is going to rain. I suspect cows lie down when they are tired.

Squirrels burying their nuts early and animals growing unusually thick coats of fur signify that a harsh winter is coming.

PLANT PREDICTORS

Going to be a bad winter? Well, in Alaska it is thought that the snow depth of the coming winter will equal the height of the current summer's fireweed. Fireweed is useful for another purpose in coastal Alaska. Natives there know that the salmon will return in time to see the fireweed bloom.

Trees keeping their leaves late into autumn foretells a bad winter.

Grape leaves turning yellow early is another sign of a hard winter coming, and sometimes a heavy crop of nuts means the same thing.

Some people believe that it's about to rain if the leaves turn their backs to the wind. Others note that many plants, including wild violets and bleeding hearts, take on a drooping aspect when a rainstorm or an electrical storm is approaching.

CONSERVING WATER

atering is one garden activity where people often get careless. A little study of how your garden responds to watering will help you become a better waterer. And with water becoming a scarce commodity in many areas, careful watering will pay dividends to both you and your garden.

CUTTING DOWN ON WHAT NEEDS WATERING

One way to cut down on watering is to minimize the area you need to irrigate. You might accomplish this by building a large deck or patio. A deck extending out from the house into the garden can be a great addition, providing extra outdoor living space. And a deck can be decorated with plants in containers, which will require some water, but that can be applied specifically and directly to the root zone. And lawns use lots and lots of water.

DROUGHT-TOLERANT GROUNDCOVERS

Many groundcovers use much less water than grass. Sedums, for example, prefer poor soil and infrequent watering. They do exceptionally well along my driveway, where the bed they are in is underlain by a rock base intended to provide support for pavement. I never expected much to grow there, and I am astonished at how happy and vigorous the sedums are.

Other drought-tolerant groundcovers that do well—and can even take some foot traffic—are prostate rosemary (*Rosmarinus officinalis prostratus*), blue star creeper (*Laurentia fluviatilis*), and several of the low-growing thymes (*Thymus* spp.). In warm climates ice plant makes a showy display. There are several ice plants—*Lampranthus*, *Delosperma*, and *Dorotheanthus* are the most common. These are natives of South Africa and suitable for Zone 9 or warmer. *Delosperma cooperi*, which bears purple flowers, is hardy to 0°F (–17.7°C), while yellow-flowered *D. nubigenum* is hardy to well below zero. It has the added attraction of green "leaves" (like green french fry wedges) that turn red in cold weather. All of the ice plants are very drought-tolerant.

WATERING WISELY

If your garden has a traditional mix of temperate-zone ornamental plants, with little drought tolerance, you can still find ways to use a lot less water than you once thought you needed.

❦

First, water the plant, not the garden. A slow-running hose with a regular sprinkler head, tucked against the base of a perennial, will do an effective job of wetting the root zone without spraying a lot of water about. When water enters soil it spreads out in a pattern similar to an inverted ice cream cone. How far to the side and how deep the water will go depends on the mechanics of the soil at the site. Water will travel more deeply than it will spread sideways. Letting a hose placed just above the root system run slowly for twenty or thirty minutes will provide enough water for a week or longer for most plants. It may take a little time to move the hose from plant to plant, but the savings in water use is worth it.

❦

If you don't want to drag a hose around, consider installing a drip irrigation system. This involves a buried hose that has emitters in place along its length; water is delivered just at the root zone, where it does the most good. Drip irrigation systems are available from garden supply stores or can be installed by a landscaper. In colder parts of the country some types may need to be taken up during the winter and set out again in spring.

A well-established shrub or tree—one that has been in the ground for a couple of years—should almost never require supplemental watering. The root system should have gone deep into the soil in that length of time. Only a prolonged and severe drought will necessitate watering—unless, of course, the plant is utterly unsuited to its habitat.

Defining Some Terms

Just What Does "Organic" Mean?

rganic is a word that means different things to different people. It is often used in advertising copy to convince consumers that a particular product is natural and healthful. The claim may even be true. But in gardener's parlance, "organic" refers to methods of growing plants without using synthetic fertilizers, manufactured herbicides, or artificially fabricated pesticides. Organic gardening is a whole philosophy that follows as closely as possible nature's own practices. Some people would define it as a biologically based, rather than a chemically based, way of sowing and growing. In organic gardening, fertilizers and pest and disease controls are made up of biological rather than chemical materials.

A plant doesn't really care whether the nitrogen it uses came out of an industrial factory or a cow. To the plant, nitrogen is nitrogen. But the "vehicle" for the nitrogen does make a difference to the soil. Mineral-based fertilizers add nutrients but do not help the soil structure, and in fact may harm it. Biologically based fertilizers also contain active organisms that improve and strengthen the soil's ability to support plant life. With the addition of organic fertilizers, soil structure is actually enhanced: worms are fed, microorganisms are preserved, and fungi are stimulated into vigor, all of which lead to healthy soil.

What Are Native Plants?

If you want to get gardeners het up, ask this simple question: What is a native plant, anyway? It may be that this innocent question causes so much difficulty because there is no truly satisfactory answer.

It does little good to say, for example, that a native plant is one that has always existed in a particular place. No plant has "always" been there. Plant species have evolved over many thousands of years, and there was a time when flowering plants did not exist anywhere. Some people hold that a native plant is one that has developed in a particular habitat and was not brought in by humans. But that definition usually refers to modern humans, or in the case of the Americas, to Europeans. Often, we have no way of knowing how a plant arrived in the place we first see it. Plants may be carried by many vehicles. Wind, animals, flooding, ocean currents, and birds all carry seeds, sometimes for very long distances. Closely related plants are found continents apart, with no real explanation.

Native Versus Alien Plants

Alien plants introduced into areas favorable for their growth, and where they have no insects or diseases to keep them in check, may wreak havoc on local plant populations. For instance, *Melaleuca quinquenervia*, the Cajeput tree, was imported to North America from Australia, and has taken over vast stretches of Florida swampland, crowding out all manner of native plant and animal life. The view Floridians have of it can be seen in its local nickname—the punk tree. For this reason, certain aggressive plants are illegal to cultivate in certain states; these plants will be unavailable at local garden centers and cannot be shipped to locations in states where they are illegal.

Much of the food we eat, however, comes from alien plants. The ordinary potato took the long way around before arriving in North America. A native of the Andes in South America, the potato was first imported to Europe. It was later brought from South America to North America by Spanish explorers. The potato made its North American landfall in St. Augustine, Florida, more than fifty years before the Puritans arrived in New England. In a strange twist, Francis Drake rescued the survivors of Sir Walter Raleigh's failed settlement in Virginia, together with some potatoes the settlers had obtained from Indians, who likely bartered them from the Spanish colonies. Those potatoes were planted by Raleigh at his estate in Ireland, thus beginning the intertwining histories of the Irish and the potato.

Even apples are not as American as apple pie. They were cultivated extensively by the Romans, who introduced them to Britain. The British brought them to the New World, where they became one of the earliest plants introduced by Europeans. Historically, apples are natives of the Caucasus mountains of west Asia, and have been cultivated there for millennia.

The lesson is that some plants have adapted well to their new homelands and fit in without outcompeting native species, while others make pests of themselves. The key is to be informed about which plants are likely to cause problems under which conditions. Investigating the plants you purchase and understanding your local ecosystem can help prevent aggressive aliens from running rampant in your garden and, worse, from escaping cultivation and destroying native plant species in your area.

ENJOYING YOUR EFFORTS

One of the best tips you will ever receive about gardening is this—practice benign neglect from time to time. Sometimes we get too involved with our gardens—we are too caring, too insistent on top performance. Or what we think of as top performance. Plants live by their own rhythm and have their own internal clocks. They did fine before people came along. So take care of their basic needs, but treat the plants in your care with a little respect. Keep your distance. The plants don't like being hovered over, picked at, and forced along.

Plant some things just for fun. If you aren't really sure what kohlrabi is or what it looks like, but you're really curious, plant a few seeds. Seeds are cheap, so experiment freely. If your tomatoes didn't do as well as you would have liked last year, and you think maybe it's time to try that trick of mulching with aluminum foil, do it. If you have an idea, try it. Fatal mistakes are rare in gardening. Some things may not work, but there's always the call of the old Brooklyn Dodgers fan—wait till next year.

HEALTH NOTES

ll gardeners should have current tetanus immunization. The tetanus bacillus can lurk in soil, especially damp soil. It usually enters the body through a break in the skin, and the wound needn't be a deep puncture in order for the bacteria to infect you; even a scratch will do it. Tetanus is rare, but is potentially fatal and completely preventable. It's not worth taking even a slight chance.

Long exposure to direct sun has been associated with the development of skin cancers, so be certain to protect yourself when you garden. Sunblock with a sun protection factor (SPF) of at least 15 is essential, as is protective clothing and a wide-brimmed hat. Apply your sunblock about twenty minutes before you go outdoors each and every time you garden, as much skin damage is cumulative.

If your skin feels dry and itchy after gardening, try my home remedy. Add a couple of cups of vinegar to your bath water. Your skin will really feel better afterward. The faint smell of vinegar on your skin dissipates in minutes.

GROWING VEGETABLES AND HERBS

DECIDING WHAT TO GROW

I have a philosophy about growing vegetables: I plant only those vegetables that can't be found locally or are superlative when eaten fresh. I now have plenty of room to grow what I want, and the first year I grew vegetables I planted a large stand of corn. I got beautiful corn, but it was a fair amount of work. Then I realized that the roadside stand a couple of miles away was selling corn for ten cents an ear. Between seed, fertilizer, and the time I spent, it was clear to me that growing corn was a bad bargain. The farmer with the roadside stand now supplies my corn, and I put my efforts into things he doesn't grow or things rarely available or expensive in the supermarket. For example, I always plant asparagus. I grow beets, and sometimes wax beans. Unusual varieties of fresh tomatoes are always a treat, and so are potatoes dug and cooked the same day.

ASPARAGUS

Once you begin to grow your own asparagus you'll see that when the stalk emerges from the ground it is as big around as it's ever going to get. Asparagus shares this characteristic with bamboo. In the supermarket, the thick stalks you see aren't necessarily any older than thin ones. Commercial asparagus growers usually harvest a stand all at once, clear-cutting everything. Thick, thin, they all get picked at the same time.

Asparagus is one of the few perennial vegetables—individual plants will produce for fifteen or twenty years, or more, but asparagus takes time to get established. In this regard, it is more like a fruit tree than a vegetable. It is best to buy one-year-old plants and let them develop their root system in your garden. While it may seem that two- or three-year-old plants would give better results, in fact they will take longer to grow strong root systems after having been dug up by the grower and replanted by the consumer. The bigger roots suffer bigger losses.

Good asparagus roots should be at least as large as a man's hand. Plant asparagus in a trench enriched with manure, compost, or other organic matter. The roots should be planted about 6 inches (15cm) deep and about 12 inches (30cm) apart, then covered with a couple of inches of soil. Gradually fill in the trench as the asparagus shoots grow, always leaving the growing tips exposed. Don't harvest any asparagus the first year, but allow it to grow into tall, feathery fronds, which will feed the establishing roots.

In cold climates, leave asparagus fronds in place until spring. The fronds hold snow, protecting the roots from extreme cold. In areas where the ground does not freeze, cut the fronds to the ground when they turn brown.

The second year you can make light cuttings of the biggest stalks—a full harvest is possible the third year. You should stop cutting when the only shoots emerging are small and thin. (Stalks of varying thicknesses come up from each plant.) Then, fertilize heavily, water well, and mulch. If manure is available, it can be used as both fertilizer and mulch.

Asparagus is best harvested by simply snapping off the stalks, leaving a bit of stalk above ground. Some people carefully cut the stalk just below the surface, and then snap the tender top off, but that's doing more than necessary and won't promote a larger yield. And do keep picking—once the stalks grow rapidly and start carrying ferny fronds, the plant thinks the year has ended and will stop producing new shoots, concentrating instead on storing energy in the roots for next year.

A bonus to growing asparagus—the roots repel wireworms and nematodes.

❧

Those little triangular things on asparagus stalks that are often trimmed off by cooks are the asparagus leaves. Well, botanically speaking, they are really scales, but they perform the function of leaves.

BEANS—GREEN AND WAX

Beans are among the easiest and most rewarding vegetables to grow. Plant the large seeds when the soil has warmed up, amending the soil with ample compost or fertilizer. Because the seeds are so large, they are especially good for kids to plant. Be careful to cover every seed or the birds will spot visible ones, and then very efficiently dig up and eat all the others you planted.

❧

One old trick calls for the gardener to dig a trench, line it with horse-hair, cover with soil, and plant bean seeds so their roots will grow down into the hair. While horsehair is reputed to be best, human hair will do in a pinch. You can tell that this tip comes from a long-gone era, when horsehair was available to most everyone. But human hair is certainly available; often barbers and beauticians will give it away by the box to an eager gardener. Hair is composed almost entirely of nitrogen, which is why the plants thrive on it.

❧

Wax beans, my favorite, should be a bright yellow when you pick them. If they still have green tinges, the flavor hasn't quite peaked.

BEETS

I set out to grow beets, and sometimes the deer feel sorry for me and leave a few. Beet tops must be one of the top three favorites of deer gourmets. It is discouraging to come out to the garden in the morning, and find bits of beet top on the ground and holes in the row. But every year I try, and sometimes defensive measures are successful. (See Dealing with Deer on page 59.)

Beets can be grown anywhere they won't get shaded by taller vegetables, and they perform well in most garden soil.

🌿

The beet seed is really three seeds in a small pod, and you must eliminate the extra seedlings, leaving only one in place at each position. Beets that only produce one plant from each seed have been developed, but these varieties seem to be disappearing from catalogs in recent years. One that is still usually available is 'Monogram'.

CARROTS

Carrot seeds are very small and rather difficult to handle. It is almost impossible to sow them as thinly as they should be, meaning mass thinning of the seedlings is required. So, give up the idea of narrow rows marching off to the horizon, and sow carrots in a wide row. Make the row as wide as you can reach across comfortably, easily a couple of feet (6m).

🌿

To scatter the seeds thinly, use the trick of mixing them with dry sand—the sand makes it easier to see where the seeds have fallen. Rake the soil lightly and firm gently with the back of a hoe or even your hand. Keep the top of the soil moist until the seeds sprout. I have found that the key to getting carrots to germinate is moisture. Drying out, even for a few hours, is fatal. A thin, thin, cover of vermiculite will hold in moisture; make it too thick and the seedlings will have difficulty pushing through.

🌿

A good cover for carrot seeds is coffee grounds, which may help keep away the carrot maggot fly. Coffee grounds also add some nitrogen, so use them sparingly. You don't want a lot of added nitrogen for carrots—it causes the heartbreak of hairy roots.

The growing bed for carrots should be carefully prepared, dug to at least 12 inches (30cm), with as many pebbles and small stones removed from the soil as possible. The carrot root will grow straight down into well-prepared soil, but will bend around an obstruction such as a pebble. Lots of small pebbles will result in amusingly shaped carrots. Larger stones may cause the root to fork.

CORN

If you really want to take the time and trouble to grow your own corn, it is a rewarding vegetable. Corn needs rich soil, ample water, and heat to grow best. Most sweet corn needs to be separated from popcorn or ornamental corn varieties if they will pollinate and mature on the same schedule; otherwise the sweet corn and ornamental corn will likely cross, with bad results for each variety. Some very new "supersweet" varieties don't need to be separated from other corns, but pay attention to planting instructions on the seed package.

Be sure to plant corn in blocks, not long rows, since corn is pollinated by wind. Planting in a close group makes for the best distribution of pollen. Improperly pollinated corn will have missing kernels on its cobs. Sometimes only a few kernels will develop if the corn plant hasn't gotten enough pollen from neighboring plants.

If you have the space and the inclination, make successive plantings of corn—early, midseason, and late. This will give you fresh corn over a long period. You can get fresh corn almost every day by staggering your planting over a two- or three-week period.

Fertilize well after the new shoots are about 6 inches (15cm) high, and again when the corn tassels begin to show. Use a balanced fertilizer, fish emulsion, or cottonseed or soybean meal.

Cultivate lightly or mulch heavily—corn roots are shallow and will be damaged by vigorous hoeing.

The flavor of the corn will be improved if the plant is kept a little on the dry side as the ear is maturing—don't parch the plant, but don't be overly generous with water either.

It used to be standard practice to pick corn, rush to the kitchen, and cook it immediately. That is still good advice for older varieties, since the sugar in corn starts to change into starch as soon as the older varieties are picked. But the newer supersweet types can be harvested over a period of a week or two, and the express trip from stalk to pot isn't necessary, since the sugar remains stable for at least several days. I think a price has to be paid for this convenience, though. The newer supersweet varieties can taste more like candy than corn.

It's almost a certainty that every once in a while you will peel back the husk on an ear and find a corn earworm busily eating away. You can adopt the organic gardener's remedy and painstakingly dab mineral oil on the silks at the tip of the ear, after the silk has begun to wither. You can also try rotenone or another chemical control. Or you can do what I do and just cut off the tip of the ear, worm and all, and use the 90 percent that's left. Corn earworms rarely go deep into the ear, and my method saves a lot of time.

After harvest, chop the stalks up and leave them on the ground as a mulch. They will break down over the winter, returning to the ground some of the nitrogen you gave them.

DILL

Dill seeds or plants can be scattered throughout the garden, anywhere there is a little space. Companion gardeners will tell you, though, not to plant dill near carrots or tomatoes because these plants are all in the same family and will attract the same pests. Dill makes good forage for beneficial insects such as damsel bug nymphs and big-eyed bugs.

Dill is easy to grow from seed but does not transplant well, so sow it where you want it. Use the young plants for fresh dill and dry some mature leaves for use over the winter.

GARLIC

Except where the ground freezes hard, garlic is planted in the autumn and harvested in June. Gardeners in cold-winter regions can plant garlic in spring and harvest in autumn. The result will be satisfactory, but the best results come from autumn planting.

Seed garlic looks just like the garlic you buy in the produce section. The individual cloves should be pulled apart and planted about 6 inches (15cm) apart in good, well-dug, well-drained soil. The end that attached to the base plate should be planted with the pointed end facing up.

Garlic might need supplemental water until autumn rains take hold. Once the weather turns cold, do not water garlic, as the plant goes into a period of very slow growth. In the spring, when growth starts again, apply a thin line of a high-nitrogen fertilizer alongside the garlic. At this point, the idea is to stimulate top growth as much and as quickly as possible. Blood meal is a good choice for fertilizer—it won't burn, is as organic as they come, and will give a quick boost to the garlic.

Further fertilization is not required. As the spring warms up and top growth seems at its peak, you can begin to hold off on water. Too much water as the bulbs are forming and enlarging can lead to soft garlic, which doesn't store well.

So-called "hard-neck" garlic varieties will send out a long shoot, which may curl around itself, forming a circle and then continuing to grow upward. This is a seed stalk, and small bulblets will form in a sack near the end of the shoot. These will take strength away from the plant, causing the garlic bulb to remain small, so trim off the bulblet sack if and as it appears. In Spain, people sauté these and then scramble with eggs for a first-rate treat.

For the last two or three weeks before you harvest, keep the garlic fairly dry to prevent the bulb from splitting. The tops will begin to droop and turn brown. At this point, bend them down to the ground. After the tops have dried out you can begin harvesting. The easiest method is to push a spading fork as deep as you can, straight down about 6 inches (15cm) from the garlic. Lift gently, and the garlic bulbs should rise enough to be retrieved. Don't pull the garlic up by the tops—that will pull the tops off and rot can enter the bulb from the damaged area.

Lay the harvested garlic on the ground to cure. If you are having cloudless days, keep the garlic in shade. After a week or so, you can rub the dirt off and store. The tops can be cut off, leaving an inch or 2 (2.5 or 5cm) of stem. Some people like to braid garlic tops for a more ornamental look, and in that case, of course, leave the tops on.

Garlic has the reputation of being an excellent neighbor in the garden and medicinal friend to people. It is reputed to repel aphids, fruit tree borers (and other borers), Japanese beetles, and plum curculio. It has a known antiseptic effect, and some think that regular eating of garlic will reduce high blood pressure. And everyone knows, or course, that it is an effective deterrent to vampires.

LETTUCE

If you have never grown common "iceberg" lettuce, you have never really tasted it. More properly called crisphead, head lettuce is a delight when you can bring it straight from the garden to the kitchen. Cool and sweet, with a satisfying crunch and snap, truly fresh lettuce is a culinary marvel. Supermarket lettuce may have been picked several weeks before it shows up in your neighborhood, and it may hang around on the produce rack for several days more. No wonder it is dry, flat, and tasteless.

When you grow your own lettuce you'll see that the plant looks quite different than it does in the store. Commercial growers trim off as many as half the leaves, leaving only the light-colored core leaves. At home you can use most of the outer leaves, which have much more flavor.

❦

I find it easiest to start lettuce in sixpacks, and then transplant seedlings to the garden. Newly emerged lettuce plants are a prime target of snails, slugs, earwigs, and who knows what else. Transplanting seedlings that are a couple of weeks old seems to deter predators. Possibly, the leaves are not quite as high in nitrogen, and thus not quite as desirable, as the brand-new leaves. Lettuce will not germinate in very warm soil, so keep the sixpacks in the shade until you see green.

❦

I have never been able to completely deter earwigs from taking up residence in head lettuce. They don't eat much, but instead seem to use the heading lettuce as a bunkhouse. If you have the same problem—I garden in an area very favorable to earwigs—here's what you can do. As soon as you cut a head, put it in a bucket of cold water. Most of the earwigs will float out. You may find others hidden in the outer leaves, and they can be easily shaken off.

❦

Head lettuce is a relatively recent development, botanically speaking, having been first cultivated during the Middle Ages in northern Europe. Leaf lettuce, on the other hand, is a very ancient vegetable. When you eat leaf lettuce you are having a treat enjoyed by Persian royalty, reserved by the Greeks for special occasions such as the coming of spring, and carried by the Romans to Britain, where it thrived.

POTATOES

It may surprise you that potatoes meet my test of growing only those vegetables that often can't be found in stores, or that are superlative when eaten fresh. It wouldn't surprise you if you ate a freshly dug boiled new potato or had a baked potato full of the flavor potatoes seem to lose in storage.

The potato bed should be well-turned and well-drained, with good organic matter levels. Compost, of course, is an excellent addition to the bed. If you need to add supplementary fertilizer, go easy on the nitrogen, which will promote large vines but few potatoes. Too much potassium can lower the protein content of the tubers. The best fertilizer for potatoes is cottonseed meal, soymeal, or any of the seed meals. Chicken manure compost can also be used.

Potatoes should be planted early, but not too early. They can be planted when the soil is workable, but may rot if planted in soil that's too cool. The soil should reach 55°F (12.8°C) at a minimum. This means that the "suggested planting date" varies from year to year. This year where I live we had almost no sun in the spring, and the soil stayed cooler than usual.

If potatoes sprout and then are nipped back by a late frost, new shoots will pop up, but yield will be reduced. Again, while the planting date will vary from year to year, a week or two before the last frost date is generally safe, since the shoots take a couple of weeks to develop and emerge. But don't overlook the fun of experimenting. Sow a few potatoes very early, and take a chance the weather will cooperate. You might well end up with some tasty very early potatoes.

The first step to planting potatoes is cutting the seed potatoes so each piece contains two eyes, which are the small dimples on the skin. Try to cut the potato so you leave as much potato as possible on each segment, since the retained moisture will ensure that the piece will sprout even if the soil dries out a little. And don't plant the end with lots of eyes. They will all sprout, but there will be so many in a limited space that they will never develop properly.

The lazy way to plant potatoes is to do it on top of the soil. It's best to bury the seed pieces about an inch (2.5cm) deep, and then mulch the row with about 6 inches (15cm) of weed-free straw or hay. You can even use grass clippings that have dried out some, but you'll need an awfully big lawn to get enough to cover a potato row with 6 inches of material. As the potatoes sprout they will come up through the straw, but most weeds won't. Add more mulch as the piles flatten out. When it's time to harvest, just pull the mulch back, and your potatoes will be waiting there, clean and easy to pick up.

Another easy way to grow potatoes is in a barrel, box, or even a clean trash can. You can have either an open bottom, with the container set above well-prepared soil, or a closed bottom with drainage holes. The open-bottomed container gives the greatest yield, but for some people the closed barrel is more practical.

Containers should be about 2×2 feet (60×60cm) or 2 feet (60cm) in diameter if round, and a convenient height, usually 3 to 4 feet (1–1.2m). You can even use fence wire to contain your mini potato patch. If you use wire, line the container with newspaper as you add soil, which will hold the soil in.

If the bottom of the container is open, place several good-sized seed pieces on the bottom and cover them with 3 inches (7cm) of mulch, well-aged compost, or even potting soil. As the vines grow, keep adding mulch or soil, covering about a third of the new top growth.

With a closed-bottom container (don't forget the drainage holes) put 6 inches (15cm) of potting soil or good mulch in the bottom and place the seed pieces on it. Then, proceed with planting as you would in an open-bottom container. Potatoes planted by either method will require supplemental watering, but keep the growing medium just damp, not dripping.

At harvest time, simply pull the container up or tip it over and pick up the potatoes. Both of these easy ways of planting generally yield enormous numbers of potatoes, as many as 20 pounds (91kg) in a 2×2×4-foot (60×60×110cm) box.

❧

Hilling up potatoes, seemingly a completely bland subject, is in fact a point of contention between two groups—the hill folk and the flat-landers. The traditional hillers recommend planting seed potatoes in a trench 6 to 8 inches (15–20cm) deep, covering the seed pieces with 3 or 4 inches (7–10cm) of soil. The seed pieces should be spaced about a foot (30cm) or a little more apart. When the sprouts appear and reach 8 inches (20cm) in height, make a hill around the sprouts with soil pulled in from both sides of the row; cover the sprouts up to the top leaves. Two additional hillings are required, about two weeks apart, but in the later hillings only add an inch (2.5cm) of soil. The point is to provide lots of loose dirt for new potatoes to form and develop. They must always be kept well covered, since if potatoes get sunburned they will turn green and produce a toxin.

The flat-landers start the same way, with trenches 6 inches (15cm) deep, covering the seed pieces with 3 inches (7cm) of soil. They let the potato stems develop to about 8 inches (20cm), and then fill in the trench to the same level as the surrounding ground, never adding any more soil around the plant. For this system to be effective the soil must be loose, not compacted by feet, so stay as far away as possible when filling in the soil and hoeing out weeds.

For either method you may need to irrigate only a little. If the soil is moist when the potatoes are planted, and if it contains lots of organic matter to ensure that the moisture will be retained, the potato plant will naturally send deep roots out and regular watering will not be necessary. A drought, of course, will mean that you need to do some supplemental watering, but water as little as possible. Dry (not bone-dry) soil produces the best-tasting potatoes. Potatoes grown in dry soil also develop thicker skins, which means they will keep better.

❧

Potatoes should be fertilized once, at about the time you are filling in your trench or hilling for the first time. The best way to fertilize is with a foliar spray, preferably fish emulsion or a liquid seaweed. This will promote rapid vine growth. Once the plants are blooming, most growth stops and the plant turns its attention to potato-making. At this point additional fertilizer won't help.

❧

You can begin to harvest potatoes when the tops begin to die down, but it's best to let the tops die back completely, and then wait a week or two. It's legitimate to sneak a few potatoes out when the blossoming is in full swing, if you do it carefully. The small new potatoes are delicious, but don't get greedy, or you won't have a main crop!

Dig potatoes when it's cool, but avoid digging them right after a rain. If the soil is fairly dry the potatoes come out cleaner. It's best to store potatoes in a cool place—dig them in the morning when the potatoes are already somewhat cool. If they do get rained on, let them dry under cover, in a single layer rather than piled up.

❧

Home gardeners rarely have to worry much about the serious scab and viral diseases that strike commercial potato growers. A good soil is the best way of avoiding disease. Hot animal manure and alkaline soil will promote disease, so don't use fresh manure or plant potatoes in alkaline soil. It's also a good idea to rotate your crops, allowing three years to go by before growing the same thing in the same place.

The Colorado potato beetle is the prime insect pest. Hand-picking is an effective control if you start when you see the first black-striped beetle. Check the undersides of leaves for small, yellow egg clusters, and rub 'em out.

A botanical note—the potato tubers will develop above the planted seed piece, on both the main stem and side shoots. Therefore, be very careful in cultivating, so you don't inadvertently slice through a baby tuber or, worse, a big one. Potatoes will not develop on roots that come out of the seed potato piece and grow downward.

RHUBARB

Rhubarb meets my test of growing something that is either unusual or difficult to find in supermarkets. You can find rhubarb for sale in the spring, but generally only for a very short time. Planting your own rhubarb will give you a much longer season—established plantings produce for a couple of months. By the time it's finished, you will probably have had your fill of rhubarb.

For planting, you buy rhubarb roots, which are available in late winter and spring. They should be kept well-watered during active growth, and respond happily to a mulch of manure or compost. Rhubarb is one of those plants that should be left to grow for a year or two before harvesting. To harvest, grasp the stalk near the base and twist off, pulling out. Don't cut with a knife or scissors or the nub will rot.

In the Deep South, grow rhubarb from seed and treat it as an annual. Plant the seed in the autumn and harvest outer stalks in the spring, the remainder in the autumn.

Rhubarb leaves are poisonous. The plant has a long history, and was used medicinally long before it was eaten or put into a pie. The ancient Chinese used dried and powdered rhubarb roots as a laxative. It was later carried by caravan to Russia, where it thrived in the cold climate. The name comes from *rha barbarum*, a combination of the Greek for the Volga river and the Roman word for foreign lands. The same Roman root word gives us "barbarian" and the lovely name "Barbara." Rhubarb was first brought to North America by Russians, who colonized the northern Pacific coast from Northern California through Alaska. Rhubarb grows very well in Alaska and is treated as a fresh fruit, eaten out of hand rather than cooked.

ANNUALS

hen most people think of flowers in the garden, they think of annuals. True to their name, annuals sprout, flower, set seed, and die in one growing season. The variety of flower shapes and forms among annuals is exceptionally wide, and they come in every color of the flower palette. They may be low-growing or tall, spreading or self-contained. Bedding plants are annuals that are set out in the spring and tilled in or mulched after being killed by autumn frost. Cutting gardens are made up chiefly of taller annuals. Extremely useful in the garden, annuals can be tucked in here and there in beds and borders, filling in anywhere a patch of bare dirt suggests that a little color would be welcome.

❧

Annuals are very easy to grow given the right cultural conditions, and usually need little care. Generally, they do well in good garden soils, require little extra fertilizer after they get established, and can grow fast enough to crowd out weeds. They do need regular watering if rains don't come, but will not thrive in soggy soil.

❧

Garden centers specialize in annuals, and will have a large selection in spring. Often, the displays appear too soon, before local conditions are right for planting. If you are over-eager to get the seedlings into the ground, you'll take a chance on being hit by an unexpected frost. These sudden frosts often come after a period of unusually warm weather but well before the established "last frost date" for your area. Annuals should be planted when the early weather has settled down and the ground has warmed up a little. Neighboring gardeners or your local extension office can tell you when it is safe to plant and avoid the last frost in your area.

❧

A worthwhile but generally unknown annual to try is *Venidium fastuosum*, a delightful flower that should be much more widely grown. It is a native of South Africa, and is fast-growing with interesting and delicate gray-green foliage on hollow, 2-foot (60cm) stems. The flowers are either a knock-your-eyes-out orange, with the petals shading to deep purple at the base, or gray-white, and both colors have large black centers. *Venidium fastuosum* comes in other colors, I understand, but I am aware of seed sources only for the orange and the white. The common name is Cape daisy, or, more poetically, monarch of the Veldt. The white form is sometimes sold as 'Zulu Prince'.

CUTTING FLOWERS

Good choices for cut flower bouquets include the many varieties of daisylike flowers—black-eyed Susan (*Rudbeckia* spp.), calendulas, China asters (*Callistephus* spp.), seed-grown dahlias, calliopsis (annual coreopsis), and cosmos. Larkspur, the annual delphinium, makes a good tall cut flower. Snapdragons, salvias, pincushion flower (*Scabiosa* spp.), and several forms of *Centaurea* (cornflower, bachelor's button, sweet sultan) add color and charm to table arrangements. The list could go on for pages—plant what's interesting and cut what you like.

❧

Sometimes you will find offered a seed package labeled as an annual cutting mix. I've had fun growing these. You aren't sure exactly what everything looks like when the plants are seedlings, so as the seeds germinate you find yourself pulling out only those things you definitely recognize as weeds. Usually, I scatter the seeds in too small an area, and have to thin severely as the plants get 6 inches (15cm) tall or so. Most grow at about the same rate, and will come into flower over a fairly short period. Last year I grew a mix that included tall marigolds, annual coreopsis, some red and pink poppies, cosmos, zinnias, and calendulas. We had interesting bouquets for weeks.

NOTORIOUS SELF-SOWERS

Some flowers throw off a lot of seeds, and these will germinate and come up the following year. Sometimes that's a real bonus. Sometimes it's not.

California poppy, for example, has a curious seedpod. After the flower drops off, the seedpod begins to elongate. It can grow as long as 6 inches (15cm), and is curved like a scimitar. The pod will dry, and when the tension on the seedpod gets to the proper point the pod explodes, splitting down the sides and throwing seeds in all directions. These poppies really pop. If you have your poppies in a garden where there is bare ground, the seeds will fall there and germinate later, either that same year, if it's early yet, or in the spring.

This trait may be either good or bad, depending on whether you are happy to have California poppies coming up randomly around your garden. I let them go. If a few pop up in inconvenient spots they are easy enough to clip off with a hoe. Otherwise, I enjoy the brilliant orange flowers dotted here and there.

One flower you should not let reseed is the four o'clock (*Mirabilis* spp.), with its pretty red, yellow, or white blossoms which open in late afternoon. Two bad things happen. Four o'clocks, while often treated as annuals, are really perennials, and during the first year develop a giant underground tuber. Volunteer flowers often revert to a muddy purplish color rather than the cheery colors of the flowers you grew from seed. So, to avoid having to dig up giant tubers all around your garden, keep four o'clocks where you put them originally, and weed out any volunteers.

Foxglove (*Digitalis purpurea*) is another flower that should not be left to run wild. It will race through the garden, and may even escape. Foxglove is highly poisonous, which may be acceptable if it grows where you can keep an eye on it. This plant is deadly to domestic animals and wildlife, so if you have a lot of either of these visitors in your garden, or if young children will be playing in the space, avoid it. Foxglove's leaves can also be mistaken for comfrey, with unfortunate results for natural food fans making what they think is a soothing tea.

One question that comes up quite a lot, it seems, is how to keep violets out of lawns. It's a question I don't understand, because I like violets in lawns, but my view is not shared by all. About five years ago at a local plant sale I spent 25 cents on a thimble-sized pot of Johnny-jump-ups and put them in my border. They have spread nicely and are a delight with their brilliant dots of yellow, lavender, and purple. Some grow in the lawn, and most stay low enough to escape the mower blade. Others pop up here and there, which I find cheerful. I suspect their seeds may be spread by birds, or maybe even by the wind. If you don't share my joy at seeing violets scattered about, they are easy enough to eliminate as they appear by pulling them out singly.

97

Corn poppy, Flanders Field poppy, or
Shirley poppy—by any name, it is a
vigorous self-sower that will take
over unprotected territory. This
habit can be turned to advantage;
if you have a sunny, out-of-the-way
area with soil that is not terribly good
try an initial planting of this delightful
flower. It will come back year after
year, and its seed may be spread
around by enthusiastic birds. As with
violas, if a few come up where they
are not welcome, the seedlings are
easily cleared away.

Calendulas will self-sow. Since they make a
fair-sized plant and are easy to recognize, it's not much trouble to pull
them out if they are a problem. However, they can act as a trap crop for
several nasty bugs, and may be an effective deterrent to some soil nematodes. Trap crops are plants grown to attract bad bugs away from more
desirable or valuable plants. Plus, of course, calendulas make fine cut
flowers, and will tolerate light frost and cold ground.

Bulbs

Growing Bulbs

Many references will tell you to add bone meal to the
planting hole when you are setting out bulbs for spring
bloom. That's a fine idea—bone meal is a slow-acting
way to add phosphorus, which is important for bulb
growth. The bone meal treatment will last for two or

three years, another advantage. But bulbs need more than phosphorus. Add a complete fertilizer, one that is either balanced among the three principal elements (nitrogen, phosphorus, and potassium) or has a higher phosphorus content. (See Fertilizing Wisely on page 10 for a more complete discussion of fertilizers.)

❧

One of the most important nutrients for bulbs to have available in quantity when they are making next year's bulb is potash, better known as potassium. Wood ashes are an excellent source of potash, and if they're available you should scatter some on your tulip or daffodil plant-ings after they bloom. You can also use the packaged potassium and magnesium sulfates sold as sul-po-mag, as well as muriate of potash.

Spring Bulb Ordering

Planning for your spring bulb display is a summer job. If you don't do your shopping in summer you'll be stuck choosing from the selection available in autumn from your local garden center. With all the thou-sands of bulbs on the market today, there are sure to be some choice beauties that they don't stock.

❧

Many mail-order catalogs carry bulbs, but several companies specialize, and some offer rare cultivars and species. (See Sources on page 150.) Generally, you will save a considerable amount of money by ordering bulbs in quantity. A hundred tulips sounds like an enormous amount, but you'll be surprised at how little space they take up. If you don't want to plant hundreds, share an order with friends and neighbors.

❧

Choosing Bulbs

Most people think of daffodils, crocus, and tulips when they think of bulbs. Broaden your horizons a little by selecting some lesser-known bulbs. Dutch iris is always a good choice. They make excellent cut flowers, blooming a little later than many bulbs and so giving you flowers

for bouquets when most of the other spring bulbs are finishing up. They come in some great colors—Wedgwood blue, lobelia blue, and blue-violet team up with yellow, white, and several bicolors to make selection difficult. And don't overlook the little iris usually called rock garden iris (*Iris reticulata*). These diminutive flowers grow only about 4 inches (10cm) tall and come in almost every shade of blue that exists, as well as in yellow and white.

There are two familiar types of anemones, *Anemone blanda*, which has starry pastel blooms, and the large Monarch DeCaens, which has broad petals in vivid colors. *Anemone blanda*, commonly called windflower, is hardy, and can be planted as far north as Zone 5. The Monarch DeCaens can be planted in autumn in areas where the ground doesn't freeze, or in the spring elsewhere. A native American anemone is *A. nemorosa*, the wood anemone, which does well in shady spots.

Grape hyacinths (*Muscari* spp.) are real delights. There are a number of cultivars, most of which have blossoms that resemble tiny clusters of purple grapes. They are short, generally 10 inches (25cm) or less, and are best planted in groups. Grape hyacinths naturalize well and form a superb front apron for taller bulbs like tulips. Another idea is to have them surround some naturalized daffodils, a yellow island in an azure sea.

Another blue charmer is scilla, or wood squill. These are also smaller plants, with only Spanish bluebells (*Scilla campanulata*) growing taller than a foot (30cm). These flowers are good for forcing, good for naturalizing, and great for the rock garden. Most are perfectly hardy, and can be planted safely in any zone; Peruvian scilla, a Mediterranean native, is tender, and should be planted out only in mild-winter areas. Siberian squill blooms very early, often coming up through snow.

Hyacinths can be grown indoors or out. The familiar Dutch hyacinths are hardy when planted outdoors and can be forced indoors, either in pots or in special hyacinth glasses. A hyacinth glass is shaped something like an hourglass—the bottom is filled with water and the bulb is placed in the top part of the glass, with the roots growing down through the neck of the glass into the water. Larger suppliers will offer hyacinth bulbs in two or three sizes, with the largest and most expensive intended for exhibition or indoor forcing and the less costly meant for bedding outdoors. A wide range of colors is available, from white to pink, red, blue, purple, and yellow—some shades are vivid while others are pastel.

BULB PLANTING AND CARE

Bulbs are some of the easiest plants to handle in the garden. When you buy them the flower is already formed within the bulb and the surrounding tissue provides all the food the flower will need. Just pop them in the ground, forget them, and in a few months you'll have great flowers!

For the best effect, plant a considerable number of bulbs in a relatively small space. The best way to prepare the planting bed is to dig out dirt to the necessary depth—usually 8 inches (20cm) for large bulbs like tulips and narcissus and 3 inches (7cm) for small bulbs like crocus. Hyacinths should be planted 6 inches (15cm) deep. Make sure the soil below planting level is loosened some, so the roots can wend their way downward easily. Work some fertilizer into the soil before you plant; mix it well with the soil so that concentrated fertilizer will not burn the first tender roots as they emerge from the bulb. Then set the bulbs in place, pointed ends up, and cover with the soil you dug out. There is one exception to the pointed-ends-up rule, and that is ranunculus. This flower has an odd tuber, composed of a cluster of many little "tuberlets." It should be planted with the points down.

❧

Allow four large bulbs and as many as nine of the smaller bulbs per square foot. If you are planting smaller quantities, space large bulbs 6 inches apart (15cm), smaller bulbs 4 inches (10cm).

❧

You can plant bulbs, especially smaller quantities, using a spade or mattock (a kind of pick that has one pointed side and one side shaped like an adz). I stopped using a bulb planter about fifteen minutes after I started using one. I was planting in fairly heavy soil, and the reputed "aid" was taking too much time and effort; making cookie cuts in the soil, then stopping to remove the soil from the tool, then replacing the soil over the bulb proved too much work for me. I went back to my spade. In loose soil, you can even use your hand to scoop out a space for the bulb.

❧

I don't like the looks of bulbs planted in straight and narrow rows (tulips and daffodils look especially stiff when planted this way). You lose a good deal of the beauty of the bulbs when they are strung out. Instead, think clusters. Plant your bulbs in groups. Smaller tulips, especially, also make a nice edging in front of taller flowers. Just don't have them standing out by themselves in a thin rank like brave rows of toy soldiers.

❧

Don't plant bulbs any closer to the surface than recommended, as they won't develop properly. In warmer climates they may emerge too soon, before the roots have made sufficient growth, and bloom close to the ground. In colder climates they may freeze.

❧

If you are cursed with gophers, as I am, you will have to adopt a special protective strategy. Bulbs, especially tulips, are the favorite food of gophers. So to protect my bulbs (and many of my perennials) I plant them in wire cages. After digging out the planting area, line the bottom with aviary wire, which has a mesh half the size of chicken wire. Lay the bulbs in place and then cover them with more wire, making sure all four sides have are fully covered. I then tie the sides of the wire together with twist ties, ensuring a solid defense with no openings. The bulb stems will come up through the wire with no difficulty.

Narcissus don't have to be caged. Narcissus bulbs are poisonous and gophers won't touch them. Or won't touch more than one.

If your ground freezes in the winter, wait until the top surface freezes, and then cover your bulb bed with a couple of inches (5cm) of mulch. It's a wise practice to save fallen leaves for this. The point is to keep the surface frozen, which is why you wait until it freezes before covering. Alternate freezing and thawing is not good for the developing bulbs.

You should have fertilized your bulbs at the time of planting. Do it twice more, once when the shoots first emerge and again when the flowers are gone and the leaves are busy making next year's bulb. If you are treating your bulbs as annuals, no fertilizing is required, since the bulb is self-sufficient for the first year.

BULB AFTERCARE

You must make a decision about what you will do once your bulb blossoms fade, and then you have to live with this choice. If you intend to keep the bulbs producing year after year, or if you are naturalizing daffodils, the foliage must stay on until it turns brown (the leaves feed the bulbs for next year's bloom). If you planted your bulbs in an out-of-the-way spot it will make no difference, but if the floppy, untidy foliage of ripening bulbs will look out of place in your garden, you might treat them as annuals, in which case you can dig them up and discard them after they have flowered. Lots of people do this.

If you are frugal and want to get several years of bloom out of your bulbs, plan how you will hide their browning foliage. One way is to plant fast-growing annuals among the bulbs, even before the bulbs bloom. It won't take anything away from the bulbs, and will dress up the plot, hiding the yellowing leaves. Some good candidates for interplanting with bulbs are marigolds, statice, the taller stocks, gaillardia, or snapdragon. Another way to go is to scatter seeds of California poppy among the bulbs in very early spring. The finely cut foliage of the poppies grows quickly, blossoms arrive soon, and the bulb foliage will melt into the background.

FORCING BULBS IN CONTAINERS

A little foresight in the autumn can bring a lot of good cheer in the dark days of late winter. A pot of spring bulbs, planted in autumn and kept in a cool dark area for three or four months, will rapidly grow and burst into bloom when brought into a warm room late in the winter. And what a cheering sight it can be, after months of dark and cold weather. There is nothing quite like a tulip to lift your spirits when you have been thinking that spring will never come. A yellow tulip opens, and hope seems possible once again.

The container you choose for forcing is important, since it will spend part of the time indoors in a decorative setting. I prefer a terra-cotta bulb pan or an azalea pot that is wider than it is tall. The pot should measure at least 6 inches (15cm) deep and 8 inches (20cm) or more across. Plastic is certainly acceptable, especially if you choose one of the newer earth tones. And plastic does have one advantage. Keeping the bulbs and soil mix damp (not wet) is crucial, and plastic holds water better than clay. Whatever container you use, make sure that it has drainage holes.

Start your bulb-forcing project in October: fill your forcing pots halfway with a very good potting soil, one that has good drainage but enough organic matter to hold some moisture. Trying to save money on the potting mix is false economy.

If you are forcing tulips, put in as many as the container will hold without the bulbs touching each other or the sides of the pot. But the bulbs should be very close. If you put the flat side of the tulip bulb facing the outside of the pot the main leaf will come up on the outer edge, giving a more complete look to the pot. And as always with bulbs (except for ranunculus), the pointed end goes up. Cover the bulbs with just enough potting mix so they are completely hidden.

Daffodils should be planted in the pots just as cozily as you would plant tulips, but the tip of the daffodil bulb can be left showing. Crocus, snowdrops, and grape hyacinths should be covered with an inch (2.5cm) or so of soil. Again, use as many bulbs as will fit in the pot without touching. And for these "minor" bulbs, choose the largest for forcing.

Most forced bulbs need three to four months of cold treatment. Cold treatment means the bulbs must be stored at temperatures below 50°F (10°C) but above freezing. In colder parts of the country a garage or an unheated porch can be a good place to keep bulbs for cold treatment. I put the pots in a large box and cover the pots with a thick layer of sawdust to make sure they don't freeze.

105

If you live where the temperature doesn't drop below 50°F (10°C) your forcing areas are more restricted. You might be able to wrangle the use of a small space in the cold room of a meat market or a university science department. Alternatively, look to buy an old refrigerator at a garage sale. A really old one with manual defrost is the best, since frost-free refrigerators have very low humidity internally and your pots will dry out unless you keep them in a sealed plastic bag.

❦

Check bulb pots in cold treatment regularly. In three months or so you will begin to see shoots poking through the potting mix. At this point you can bring the pots into a warmer area, and allow them to have some light. After the bulbs show some real growth, it's time to bring the pot into your living area, so you can see the developing flower emerge and open. Usually the flowers will last a week, or a little longer if you keep the area fairly cool. Warm room temperatures will reduce the time the blooms remain fresh-looking.

❦

Paperwhite narcissus (look for the popular cultivars 'Soleil d'Or', 'Cragford', and 'Galilee') don't require a cold, dark treatment. Pot them up and they will bloom in four to six weeks. If you order a quantity you can pot them throughout the winter for a succession of blooms.

❦

For a unique finishing touch, add some seeds to your forcing pot once you bring it into a warmer area. The seeds will sprout, making it look as if the bulb is growing naturally outdoors. Grass seed is often recommended for this, but I find that it looks odd. Newly emerged grass is very thin and fine, and to my mind it just doesn't work indoors. Instead, try wheat. Where do you find wheat seeds in small quantities? Certainly not in the usual catalogs. You find wheat seeds in health food stores, where they are sold as wheat berries or wheatgrass. This is just regular old wheat—it will sprout in a few days and has a leaf much wider and more substantial than grass. And for some reason, perhaps due to the limited space in the pot, the wheat will not get as tall as your tulips until well after they have blossomed.

Another idea for filling out your bulb pot is to use chia seeds, the same type of salvia seeds used in Chia Pets. As far as I know, they are only available from J.L. Hudson (see Sources on page 150). They sprout quickly and will soon cover the surface.

ROSES

SOME ROSE TIPS

oses are a vast and complex subject. If you are deeply interested in them, consider joining a local rose club, the American Rose Society, or another enthusiasts' organization. One way to locate other hobbyists is to visit country fairs that feature floral competitions—rose gardeners are sure to be in attendance and eager to share information with a novice.

Following are a few tips for growing healthy roses.

Banana peels make an excellent fertilizer for roses. Cut the peels into small pieces and bury them a couple of inches (5cm) deep in the soil around the rose bush. The peel is high in potassium and potash, and is a treat for the rose. Don't put more than three banana peels beneath a bush, as you don't want to push too much of a good thing.

When buying roses, look for those labeled Number 1 grade. These will have the best-developed root system and the strongest canes. Grade 1½ can be acceptable if the color and cultivar you want is only available in that grade. A Grade 2 rose will take several years to establish, and may never get as vigorous as a rose of a better grade.

Modern hybrid tea roses are grafted (or budded) onto a rose root stock selected for its vigor and ability to support a large top, but which does not itself have attractive flowers. The bud union can be easily seen; it appears as a swelling just above the roots. If you find a branch growing out of the bud union or from the trunk below it, prune the branch off. It will have the less attractive characteristics of its parent.

When cutting roses to bring into the house for display, slit the bottom of the stem an inch or two (2.5 or 5cm). This will allow the rose to draw water easily and keeps the blooms fresh longer. It was once thought that crushing the bottom of the stem was helpful, but that has been disproved—slitting is all that's necessary. Preparing the stem in this way is a good practice for any flower with a thick, woody stem.

Multiflora roses planted in a row can make an attractive and very effective natural fence. As the plants mature they can be pruned to shape.

PRUNING ROSES

I used to fret over pruning roses. I was very afraid that I would make a mistake and kill the plant or leave an obvious sign that I didn't know what I was doing. Well, it's not really that hard or that dangerous.

The reason for pruning is to stimulate vigorous new growth, since most roses bloom on new wood, although some species, shrub, and old garden roses bloom on older wood. The best time to prune is at the end of the rose's winter dormancy (see A Special Note on Climbers on page 109).

This usually comes at the end of the coldest part of the year, January in mild climates to mid-March in the coldest areas. When I lived in coastal California I pruned the week between Christmas and New Year's, which worked out well. When I was growing up in a cold climate my father pruned close to Easter, and that was successful, too. A very late Easter might call for pruning around two weeks before.

❧

You also need to know *how* to prune. In cold climates you must check the rose plant and cut out any canes that have been winter-killed. This may leave only stubby remnants, but that's okay, the rose will recover. In more temperate regions, you won't need to worry about winterkill. You should always cut out crossing stems, for you want to have an open center for good air circulation. Good movement of air will deter some of the problems common to roses, especially mildew. When you prune, also trim off weak outer branches, for they will never develop into strong bearers of quality blooms.

Once you've cut out dead and weak canes, cut the whole plant down by about a third, or even by one half in warmer climates where growth is strong. This is not a complicated process. Growth buds, little swelling nubs, are evident on the stems, and you should cut just above outer-facing buds. Inner-facing buds will turn into crossing branches, clogging up the center. Make your cuts on a slant so that rainwater will slide off the stem end. Clean up all old leaves and broken branches around the shrub, as well as the prunings, to minimize the spread of disease. And, as always, make sure to use sharp pruning shears. Dull blades crush the stem ends, leaving a surface that invites diseases to enter.

As you work, step back every so often to check your progress. Even if you cut a little too much on one side, new growth will fill in any mistakes, and you will have learned something in the process.

A Special Note on Climbers

There are two different types of climbing roses—those that bloom once in the spring and those that have two or three bloom periods during the year. All climbing roses should be allowed to grow without pruning for their first two or three years so that the plants can establish themselves and develop their characteristic long canes.

Climbers that bloom repeatedly may be pruned during dormancy, as you would with most roses, since they are likely sports of hybrid tea roses. Prune once-blooming roses after they have stopped flowering. They will bloom again next spring on the strong new growth that begins after pruning.

LAWN CARE

grass lawn is a very strange place, when you think of it. Unlike any other part of your garden, or anything in nature, it is an area of closely packed identical plants. People grow grass lawns in a way they grow no other plant. And it is possible to do this because grasses, both warm-season and cool-season varieties, are very tough plants. But they will do much better if you put some effort into preparing the lawn area beforehand, so the grass plants have the best conditions you can give them.

DECIDING WHETHER TO INSTALL A NEW LAWN

Installing a new lawn, either from sod or seed, is a major undertaking, but one that will pay off for years if done right. While I find vast expanses of unrelieved green grass rather dull, a lawn can be an integral part of a well-designed landscape. There is no better groundcover than grass. It cools and cleans the air in exactly the same way a tree does, but without the drama. Grass makes a safe and comfortable play space for children and an ideal entertainment area for you.

❧

First you need to decide if it makes sense to put in a new lawn, and if it does, whether to seed or sod. If you have a new house surrounded by bare soil and remnants of construction, a new lawn is a necessity. But if your lawn is less than what you would like to have, or if you inherit an inferior lawn with the house you buy, you'll have to judge the best approach. One school of thought maintains that if your lawn has at least 50 percent good grass, renovate rather than starting afresh. Another expert says you need to have only 30 percent good grass, and can help along the rest with the proper soil amendments, fertilizers, and seed. This means it's really up to you. Renovating may not be quite as much work as establishing a completely new lawn, but it's still a substantial effort. Starting over may even be easier, as you can just go ahead and clear, improve, grade, fertilize, and so forth in a single operation, rather than doing all the same things here and there, between good areas of existing grass.

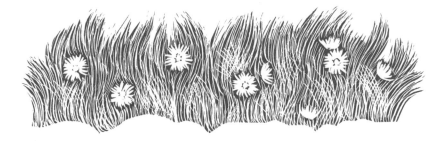

Preparing for a Lawn

If you have the remnants of an old lawn to deal with, you have some work ahead of you. It's not a good practice to rototill in the old lawn. That results in a seedbed for the new lawn that is irregular and filled with air pockets and impenetrable clumps—generally a bad way to start a lawn. Power equipment, either a sod cutter or a power rake, can be rented to eradicate the old turf, weeds and all. A sod cutter does just that, leaving clean dirt. Depending on your local conditions and grade, you may then need to add some top soil. Buy the best you can; that's the most economical way because it will result in a better lawn for years to come. If you use a power rake you will have to rake up the remnants, which compost easily.

❧

The best time to start a new lawn is the autumn. It's always best to follow nature's example, and grass goes to seed in late summer, with the new grass germinating in the early autumn rains. The process of starting a new lawn from seed will take about six weeks, so begin your preparations with that in mind: time the seeding to occur when the air has cooled from the heat of summer, the soil is still warm, and rain is due.

🌿

Whether you are sodding or seeding, the initial preparations are the same. You need to kill off existing vegetation, deal with the weed seeds that are going to be there, test the soil's fertility, till or dig the soil up, remove debris, add amendments as needed, add fertilizer, smooth the area, and seed or sod. Once the seed or sod is in place, the tasks become different. Seed needs much more care for another month or so, while sod is lower maintenance.

Once you have removed any existing grass, test the soil to see if you need to add nutrients or adjust the pH (see Testing for Nutrients on page 9 and Changing the pH of Your Soil on page 11). Almost certainly you will need to add something, and several amendments may be recommended. I'd take these recommendations seriously. Once the lawn is in place it will be more difficult to change the soil composition.

🌿

After clearing the surface and testing the soil, the lawn area should be rototilled deeply to establish a loose and receptive base for grass to root. Do a rough grading, to make sure the lawn area slopes away from the house slightly, so water will not collect around the foundation. You don't need much of a grade, just 1 or 2 percent, or a drop of 1 to 2 feet (30cm to 60cm) over a length of 100 feet (30m), or 3 inches (7cm) every 10 feet (3m).

At this time fertilizers and soil amendments can be tilled in as well. The basic tilling should be done as deeply as the tiller will go, and that probably means you will have to make several passes; the first will be fairly shallow and the next will till deeper. In the final pass, amendments and fertilizer can be tilled in. At this point, get the bed roughly smooth and water it. The next step is to germinate all those weed seeds that are waiting just under the surface.

Give the weeds three or four weeks to germinate, then till again, but this time very shallowly. This will chop up the new weeds, but will not bring new seeds to the surface. This simple step can save hours of weeding later. If it's not possible to till again, rake well to destroy the weeds. Once you've tilled or raked out all the newly germinated weeds, rake again, this time getting the seedbed as smooth and level as possible. Some gardeners drag a doormat or something similar over the area, to highlight low spots. Finally, go over the seedbed with a roller that is either empty or only partially full, since you don't want to compact the soil too much.

CHOOSING A GRASS

Let's talk a bit about the various kinds of grass seeds there are. People in most parts of North America will sow cool-season grasses, and the grass breeders have been very busy lately. Not so long ago the selection was limited to Kentucky bluegrass, ryes both annual and perennial, and a fescue or two. In recent years a whole new array of grasses, especially tall fescues, have been developed, and these make superior lawns. While they are slightly coarser than the finest bluegrasses, the new varieties of tall fescues stay green all year round and grow well with considerably less water than bluegrass needs. In what seems like an oxymoron, dwarf tall fescues that need less mowing have been introduced. What a bonanza! These grasses also need less water and stay green all year round.

There are advances being made in warm-season grasses, as well. A new hybrid Bermuda uses a lot less water than older types. The warm-season grasses, such as the Bermudas and St. Augustine grass, are usually planted from stolons or plugs rather than from seed.

Choose lawn seed that includes a mix of varieties. This is a little more prudent than planting seed of a single type, as a mix will adapt better.

Some seeds will do better than others, and over time the ones best adapted to your special circumstances will outcompete the rest. A lawn composed of different types of grass will be better able to handle stressful conditions. If you plant a single seed type and it happens to be one not well-adjusted to drought, for example, you run the risk of having the whole lawn die in a dry year.

A box of grass seed will list the percentages of the various seeds it contains. Note that the percentages are by weight, not by amount of seed, which can be misleading. Coarse grasses that grow fast but don't look as nice as finer grasses have larger seeds, and therefore will grow fewer plants per pound than premium grasses with finer seeds. Even though finer-bladed seeds will cost more per pound, they have many more seeds per pound, so the same weight will cover a larger area. The last place you want to economize is with the seed. You are making a lawn forever, or that should be your philosophy, and better seed will make a better lawn.

SEEDING AND AFTERCARE

The amount of seed you need will depend on the blend. The package will tell you how much seed will be required for the area of your lawn.

You can broadcast the seed by hand, taking care to cover all the ground evenly with seed. It's not as difficult as you may think, and works pretty well on a windless day. But don't even try it in wind. The other option is a mechanical seeder, a V-shaped tub on wheels that has calibrated openings to allow seed to fall through onto the ground as you push it along.

Measure the seed before you begin, and sow in one direction using half the seed required. Next, sow in the other direction, across the first pass to ensure even distribution. Be careful at the end of a row and during turns, since it's easy to allow too much seed to be laid as you turn the seeder.

114

Some gardeners cover the seed with a light mulch. A *very* light mulch. This can help the seedbed stay moist until the seed germinates. If the mulch is too heavy, some seed will not germinate and some will come up in blotches, so be sure to use a light hand. Aged compost or soil conditioner can be used as a mulch, or you can use pulverized peat moss. Some gardeners use straw, which is okay, but it must be applied very thinly so you can still see mostly bare soil.

After the seed is sown, you can either roll again lightly to make sure the seed has made firm contact with the soil, or you can rake lightly, so most of the seed falls into tiny trenches. Next, water. From now until the seeds germinate and you have a good green cover, it's necessary to keep the seeds moist. Moist doesn't mean soaked. Usually you will have to water lightly three or four times a day. If you encounter a spell of cool and cloudy weather you won't have to water as often. Warm windy weather, on the other hand, will really dry out the soil quickly, and frequent sprinklings will be necessary. This, incidentally, is the only time I recommend light sprinkling. In most cases watering is best done deeply and thoroughly, for both lawn and garden.

Depending on the seed you planted, you will have to continue light, frequent watering for several weeks, until most of the seed has sprouted. It will sprout over time, so don't stop watering when you first see some little grass shoots. There are more to come.

You may begin to see weeds after a week or so, even if you tried to get them all before you seeded. Anything you see sprouting that's not a fine-bladed grass, pull now. If the weeds are too far away to reach, leave them until the grass can take some foot traffic. You can lay a board down and kneel on that to extend your reach to some extent.

When should you mow for the first time? Don't be in too much of a hurry. I'd wait until the grass is between 3 and 4 inches (7 and 10cm) tall, then mow high, setting the mower for 3 inches. With new grass it's better to mow frequently than to let the grass get too high or to scalp it. Another way to tell it's time to mow is when the grass stops standing straight up and begins to curve.

Sowing Stolons or Sprigs

If you are sowing stolons or sprigs, you have a much easier job. Many of the warm-season grasses are sold this way. Stolons are the easiest of all. You just need to broadcast them over the lawn, roll it, and water. You may want to use some mulch over the stolons before the final rolling and watering. Your supplier will advise you on the number of stolons needed for your lawn area.

Plant sprigs, or plugs, of grass the same way you plant anything from a sixpack. Using a trowel, make depressions, put in the sprigs, and fill in with soil. Again, your supplier will tell you the recommended number of plants and spacing you will need to make a good lawn.

Sodding

The quick way to get a lawn is to use sod. Your lawn area should be prepared in the same way as for seed, with one exception (see Preparing for a Lawn on page 111). You must allow for the height of the sod. So, where the sod will abut a sidewalk or driveway, or edge a planted island, lower the seedbed, now called the sod bed, by the thickness of the sod, about 2 inches (5cm) or so. Don't be too concerned about the space you leave, since over time things will even out, but at the beginning you don't want the sod to be riding high out of the water like a too-light sailboat.

Be ready for the sod when it's delivered. It will be cut to order at the sod farm and brought to you in rolls. If the rolls are left for days, they will heat up internally, dry out externally, and turn into an ugly sight. If you can't install the sod for a day or two, try to have it off-loaded in a shady area and keep it moist.

Installing sod is one of the easiest gardening jobs you will have, once the sod bed is properly prepared. Just roll the sod out, making sure it makes tight contact on all sides, either with other sod, header board, or pavement. It is sometimes recommended that you stagger the ends so you don't get obvious seams, but I haven't found seams to be a problem. The edges of the sod will knit together quickly enough if they are butted tightly together.

Once sod is laid, water thoroughly. Keep watering until the roots of the sod have grown down into the underlying soil. You don't need to flood it, but you do need to make sure that water is getting all the way through the sod. Do this by looking—just lift gently and peek under an edge to see if it's moist. When you can no longer lift the sod to peek, it's knitted into place.

You can mow sod earlier than you would seed-sown grass. High mowing gives the best results. A newly sodded lawn can start into growth quickly, since the sod is already living and growing when you put it in place.

MOWING

It may be logical to think that if you mow your grass short, you will have to do it less often. In fact, the physiology of the grass plant leads to the opposite situation. If you mow high, cutting off no more than a third of the grass, you leave plenty of growing area on the grass plant, and it will grow moderately. If you cut too short, only a little growing area is left, and the plant compensates by speeding up the growth process. So, you will have to mow sooner. If you do this on a regular basis, you weaken the grass that's left by putting it into repeated cycles of frantic growth. Mow high, and you will mow less, especially in the summer. The cool-season grasses, like bluegrass, fescue, and perennial rye, will go semi-dormant in midsummer, and won't grow much, even if they stay green.

In the spring your lawn will grow on its own, responding to warmer air and brighter, longer days. The lawn should always be cut with the mower blades set high, about 3 inches (7cm) or so. This is a good height for the grass itself. Cutting the grass close to the ground cuts off its growing area, and results in browning. And most lawn weeds are low growers, so leaving the grass high shades out weeds, helping in your weed control battle.

FEEDING THE LAWN

If you have a good healthy lawn, spring fertilizing is not necessary. I know, I know, every garden center promotes spring fertilizer. It's good for the fertilizer companies. But a lawn in good condition will grow well without extra stimulation in the spring. If you have just moved to a new home and the lawn has lots of weeds in it, you can go ahead that first spring with a weed and feed program, to help get things under control. But proper lawn maintenance will result over time in a lawn that pretty much takes care of itself as far as growth and weeds go. The following tips are for lawn fertilizing in most of North America, except in the humid Deep South and the arid Southwest. They apply to the "cool season" grasses—the fescues, bluegrass, and perennial rye that make up the lawns in most parts of North America. (See also Fertilizing Lawns in Hot Climates on page 119.)

The best fertilizer for your lawn is your lawn. Leave the grass clippings on the lawn to break down naturally, releasing their stored nutrients, especially nitrogen. If the grass has gotten a little high and the clippings

118

are heavy and matting, rake them off and use them in your compost pile or as a mulch elsewhere in the garden. But for the most part, let your lawn feed your lawn. You may have heard horror stories about the dreaded thatch. Thatch is bad stuff, dead clippings on the surface that dry out and prevent water and air from getting into the soil. But thatch is actually the result of a biologically dead lawn, killed by chemical fertilizers and weed killers rather than clippings.

Artificial fertilizers are a problem everywhere in the garden but they can be devastating to the lawn. Strong chemical fertilizers stimulate root growth close to the ground's surface, where the roots are vulnerable to dying the first time the weather gets hot and dry. These fertilizers also kill normal soil microorganisms, so their job of breaking down grass clippings is not done. If you use harsh fertilizers, then worms, your lawn's best friend, won't come to the surface and eat the grass clippings, processing them into beneficial humus. Chemical fertilizers are a losing proposition all the way around.

In a lawn that's biologically alive the grass clippings are transformed into humus; the soil is kept loosened and porous by earthworms; roots grow deep, looking for the water that penetrates well below the surface; and the grass stays green and healthy even when rain or irrigation is sparse.

FERTILIZING LAWNS IN HOT CLIMATES

Gardeners in the Deep South have different grasses and different requirements. The plants most often used for lawns in the South are St. Augustinegrass, Bahiagrass, Bermuda grass, buffalo grass, and sometimes centipedegrass and zoysia. Warm-season grasses should be fertilized on a different schedule than cool-season ones. If you live in a dry area and don't irrigate, fertilize your lawn in April and again in August. If you do irrigate regularly, fertilize in light amounts every month from April or May through Labor Day. In the Deep South, fertilize in June and again around Labor Day.

If your lawn is made up of warm-season grass, which goes dormant and turns tawny in the winter, you may wish to overseed with a cool-season grass, such as Kentucky bluegrass or rye. If you do decide to plant some cool-season grass, you should fertilize in early autumn, just like the rest of the country.

Patching a Lawn

If you have large bare spots or areas where all the green is weeds and no grass grows, take care of these areas in the spring. To do this, remove the weeds or bad grass and spade the ground. I use a spading fork, which will both dig up the old vegetation and loosen the soil without compacting it. Next, dig in some compost or peat moss. If you use peat moss, and this is one of the few times it makes sense to use it (peat is a nonrenewable resource, so should be used sparingly), make sure it is thoroughly mixed with the dirt. Otherwise, the peat moss can dry out and become impervious to water, resulting in a permanent desert area in your lawn. An insider's tip—add some used coffee grounds now. New grass loves coffee. I sprinkle coffee grounds around just before I use the spading fork. You don't need a lot: the coffee grounds shouldn't be visible after you work the soil.

Sprinkle new grass seed on the soil, but not too thickly. Think of it as if you are salting food. Rake the seed in, barely covering it with soil. Finish with a light mulch of fine soil conditioner or compost sprinkled over the seed—use a very light hand. A dusting of mulch will help keep the dirt damp, but too much will smother the seed, making it come up in an unattractive blotchy fashion—or not come up at all.

The seeded area must be kept moist until the seeds sprout—it may need three or four daily dampenings with a fine spray until the new grass sprouts, usually in five days or so, but it will take a little longer if the soil is still cold.

Watering the Lawn

Summer is the time lawns get stressed, from heat, from drought, and from use. You should continue to mow high. This is healthier for the lawn, since it leaves the grass with more of the food-producing leaf area intact. Watering is another matter.

❧

Lawns were made popular in the eastern part of North America by people who knew them in their native Britain and Ireland. With their year-round rainfall, Britain and Ireland are great places for lawns. So is the eastern part of the United States, most years. But out beyond the Hundredth Meridian water starts to become scarce, leading to the question: Should I water my lawn?

This question may seem odd to people who have grown up with green grass and water hoses. Of course you water your lawn in the summer. It's one of the rituals of life. But it's a whole different thing where it doesn't rain in the middle of the year. Even the moist Pacific Northwest turns off the rain spigot in the summer. Seattle gets less than 2 inches (5cm) of rain on average in the summer. Portland, where people can develop webbed feet during most of the year, only gets a $1/2$ inch (1cm) total in July and August. In most of California it barely rains at all from May through September.

It seems to me a given that if you live in a desert area, Arizona, for example, a New England–style lawn is out of the question. It's both well-known and sad that the desert climate and pure air that people came to Arizona for has been seriously compromised by the pollens of the plants immigrants landscaped with, I guess to remind them of the places they left behind. And those plants all need to be watered regularly, using a resource that is becoming increasingly scarce. It makes no sense at all to also expect to have a lot-line to lot-line lawn, just like the one left back home in Indiana.

I'm an advocate of letting lawns go dormant during the western summer. If I still lived in Western New York, I'd say water. There, dry spells come every year, and while grass, especially well-grown healthy grass, can take a surprising amount of dryness, it's best not to force them into a premature dormancy, only to be stimulated again by early autumn rain. That way you can get too much tender new growth just before really cold weather sets in, and that's not a good idea.

We tend to water too much—it's a good thing for lawns to go dry occasionally. It forces the roots of grasses to go deep, searching for moisture. Some diseases can be lessened by avoiding excess watering. And some weeds will not be able to compete in a drier lawn. In the moister parts of the country lawns need something on the order of an inch (2.5cm) of rain a week, or 12 inches (30cm) over the course of a summer. Rain usually doesn't come evenly, so supplemental watering may be required if a few weeks have passed with no rainfall.

Your lawn will give you clues when it's getting too dry. Walk on the lawn. Normally, footprints will disappear after a short time. If you still see footprints where you have walked on a lawn several hours before, it's time to water. If the grass begins to look dull, slightly hazy, it's time to water.

Always water deeply. Water slowly enough that there is little or no runoff onto sidewalks or streets. Water early in the day, so the grass has a chance to dry off before nightfall. Watering in the middle of a sunny day means that as much as half the water evaporates before penetrating into the soil. On a windy sunny day the waste is even worse.

Measure the amount as you water. Any container with a fairly wide opening will do—a coffee can, for example. Simply set the can on the lawn within the range of the sprinkler. Many sprinklers spray water unevenly, so it's best to use several cans to measure in different locations. When you have an inch (2.5cm) of water in the can, you have given the lawn an inch (2.5cm) to an inch and a half (4cm). Sandy soil will need a little more water, since it is a bit more porous. Clay soil will need less water, but if you start to get runoff, stop for half an hour or so to let the water soak in, then apply more. In dry conditions, gardeners often believe that muddying of the surface soil means that the plants have gotten enough water, when in fact the roots are still dry. A little experience will tell you how long to water.

LAWN WEEDS

Summer is the time when weeds become more prominent. In the spring, the grass is growing quickly and the weeds are less noticeable. By the time summer comes, the weeds may have caught up and now stand out.

Good lawn care practices can be very effective in curbing some weeds. Mow high, for starters. Higher grass, about 3 inches (7cm) or so, will shade many weeds, and any plant deprived of sun will weaken and eventually die. Let the lawn go a little dry. If you adhere to a rigid plan of watering, you will only be encouraging weeds, and will probably be giving the grass more water than they need. Also, modify your watering to account for rain.

Pull your weeds. That's a most effective way to get rid of them! It's easiest when the soil is a little damp. Then, weeds will come out of the ground with less effort on your part. There are some weeds that demand weeding. Bindweed, the evil cousin of morning glories, is particularly difficult to eradicate. You will see a morning glory sort of flower, with a small leaf or two and a wiry stem. What you see is the very top part of a plant, which may have a 20- or 30-foot (6 or 9m) root system that extends far from where you see the flower. Cut off the visible weed and another will sprout nearby. Be patient and keep pulling the weed. No root system can exist forever if there are no leaves to photosynthesize and provide food. Just keep hacking off what you see; you will begin to see fewer of the flowers and eventually you will have killed it.

Bindweed will be happiest in the garden on bare dirt, and will be hardest to control there. In a lawn, constant vigilance combined with high mowing will help control bindweed.

The key to dealing with dandelions is to keep them from flowering and setting seed. They prefer poor soils, so enriching your lawn will help to get rid of them. And dandelions have very pretty flowers. A few can be kind of decorative. So can a bunch. One day I drove past an abandoned farm, and what had been the front lawn was a solid tapestry of yellow. Some gardeners would work hard to get such an effect. Don't obsess about a few. Dandelions can be pulled or dug out with a special narrow-shafted tool, but you need to get most of the root, or it will sprout again.

Some people look on clover as a weed. It's actually a useful plant in a lawn, providing extra nitrogen to the grass. It's not strongly competitive, and having a little is a good thing. Some gardeners sow clover seed to ensure extra nitrogen for grass. But there is a type of clover you should try to eliminate. The flower is yellow and the plant sends out long shoots, which root at the joints and can quickly form a mat that chokes out grass. Or, rather, it chokes what grass is remaining, since yellow clover, some-times called black medic, grows best in poor, nitrogen-depleted soils that don't have the characteristics to make a good lawn. If you have black medic, fertilize generously with an organic lawn fertilizer high in nitrogen. You will soon see fewer tiny yellow flowers and more grass. Burclover is very similar to black medic, and is treated the same way.

One lawn problem associated with a lack of nutrients in the soil, among other things, is moss. Moss doesn't crowd out grass, it takes over where grass is weak or nonexistent. Moss is usually the result of poor nutrition, too much shade, poor drainage, and/or soil that is too acidic. Liming can raise the pH of very acidic soil, but you don't want to raise it much beyond 6 or 6.5. Grass likes a little bit of acidity. Feed your lawn in the autumn, eliminate some shade by pruning if possible, and try to improve drainage if the mossy area always stays wet.

Crabgrass is the bane of otherwise sensible people. The annual battle against crabgrass, or witchgrass, or whatever its called where you garden consumes many hours, much effort, and not a little money. It does really well in warm damp soil, and so is a particular pest on the East Coast, with the emergence of crabgrass following the sun northward. The best controls are mechanical. Pull new shoots whenever you see them. A lawn in vigorous growth will provide tough competition for crabgrass, so mow high and don't let it go to seed in the autumn; be especially watchful in ornamental plantings, since crabgrass can sprout a flower unnoticed away from the lawn.

Other weeds that bedevil the gardener are chickweed, purslane, and plantain. The most effective treatment is pulling them up and digging them out. Chickweed and purslane are annuals, and you will see them disappear eventually if you keep them from flowering and setting seed. The best approach is to grub them out whenever you spot them. Plantain is a perennial, but if you keep it from reseeding it, too, will begin to disappear.

WEED-KILLER RECIPE

This recipe is useful for any sort of weed, but use caution when applying it, as it will kill or seriously damage any plant it wets.

> **Ingredients**
> *1 gallon (4.5l) white vinegar*
> *1 cup (250ml) table salt*
> *1 tablespoon (15ml) dishwashing liquid*

Combine the white vinegar, salt, and dishwashing liquid and shake well to mix thoroughly. Use in a hand sprayer on weeds. It may also be applied with a brush directly to the weed, to minimize overspray. Use the kind of dishwashing liquid you use in a dishpan, not the kind used in dish-washing machines. This formulation will act quickly, turning the sprayed leaves brown or gray almost immediately. However, new shoots may well appear in a few days, so repeated applications may be necessary. Because of the salt content, flush the area with water a few days after you are sure the weeds are dead. This weed killer should not be used in arid climates where the salt will accumulate.

Establishing a Grassless Lawn

A recent popular way to achieve low maintenance and water conservation at the same time is the grassless lawn, or rather, the turfless lawn. Landscaping without the traditional grass lawn can yield very attractive results. But you should be aware that low maintenance doesn't mean no maintenance, water conservation doesn't mean eliminating watering completely, and grassless landscaping can involve a whole lot of work at the outset.

To be successful the grassless lawn must be attractive. Scattering some wildflower seeds and then walking away won't give you a beautiful meadow. It will give you a weed-choked yard that will drive your neighbors nuts. If you want a wildflower "meadow," make sure that you are gardening in a location where that sort of planting won't look out of place. A meadow doesn't look natural on a small urban lot. But if you create a plan that incorporates distinct areas seeded with wildflowers together with some "hardscape" elements—stones, rocks, or decorative concrete even—you can make your yard the envy of the neighborhood.

An Ornamental Grass Garden

Instead of a traditional lawn, you may choose to create a garden of ornamental grasses, both tall and short, which bring color and texture to the scene. Ornamental grasses have become increasingly and deservedly popular recently, and the modern selection is wide. Some are even carried by large garden super stores, but if you really want to have the widest selection, get catalogs from specialty growers (see Sources on page150).

In addition to the standard lawn fescues, there are several attractive ornamental fescues, including *Festuca glauca*, *F. mairei*, (Atlas Fescue, a very tough plant with light gray-green leaves), and *F. valesiaca glaucantha*, a neat, small clumper that spreads only 6 inches (15cm). The cultivar of

126

F. glauca 'Elijah Blue', is especially attractive, with a mounding habit and steel-blue leaves.

Miscanthus sinensis comes in several forms, and generally grows to 6 feet (1.8m) tall or more, often with variegated leaves. The pennisetums are usually lower-growing, with autumn color and coppery flowers.

One special type of ornamental grass is sedge, with the botanical genus name *Carex*. The sedges look a lot like ordinary lawn grass, can be mowed or left to grow naturally, and are available in types that like wet areas or are drought-tolerant. This flexible and adaptable family should be grown in more gardens, since it is both attractive and unusual.

Shrubs

Rhododendrons

hododendrons and azaleas (both in the genus *Rhododendron*) are the aristocrats of the garden. If you live in the Pacific Northwest, where rhododendrons grow wild and bloom boisterously, you know how truly impressive they can be. But they do require specific conditions—acidic soil and moist, cool air—that are not possible everywhere. Azaleas are much more adaptable, at least as far as temperatures go. Rhododendrons are more associated with cooler northern climes, while azaleas are a southern star.

Rhododendrons need acidic soil, and so should be fertilized with a high-nitrogen fertilizer. In the garden, regular feeding with a liquid fertilizer is the usual practice, but be careful with fertilizer when the temperatures are high, since the roots can be burned. Make sure you feed rhododendrons in the spring as the plants are blooming, as soon as the flowers fade, and again in early autumn. Those are the crucial times for the shrub, and will ordinarily be sufficient.

🌿

Prune when the plants are in flower, cutting some to bring into the house. And prune off spent flowers after bloom. Most rhododendrons need only light pruning for shape. If your plant needs severe pruning, be prepared to sacrifice some of this year's growth, and prune early in spring, just as growth starts.

🌿

Azaleas need much the same conditions as rhododendrons. Acidic soil is a must, as is high moisture content in the soil and the air. Don't drown the shrubs, but keep them moist and make sure they have good drainage. Tip pruning—pinching off the end growth of a branch— will encourage bushiness and fullness. It's best to tip prune right after flowering during the period of active growth early in the summer. This will encourage both compactness and maximum flowering the following year.

PRUNING SHRUBS

Shrubs that flower in the spring, such as lilacs, should be pruned right after the flowers fade. They are also "pruned" when the gardener cuts branches to bring indoors. Lilacs will give the best flowers year after year if all the branches or shoots with faded blossoms are trimmed away. It's best to do this early, since lilacs flower on the previous year's growth, with the flower buds forming at the ends of new shoots. Never prune a lilac in autumn, as you'll be cutting off next year's flowers.

Shrubs that bloom in the spring have growth and flowering patterns like lilacs. Other shrubs include flowering quince, forsythia, winter hazel, India hawthorn, weigela, and some spiraeas and viburnums. Shrubs that bloom in the summer on new growth, such as buddleia, better known as the butterfly bush, caryopteris, potentilla, and oleander, are best pruned during winter dormancy.

There are two basic pruning cuts: heading and thinning. Heading—cutting the ends of branches—results in a sheared appearance, at least at first. It is attractive for certain plants, such as boxwood, arborvitae, some junipers, and pyracantha. In general, the fine-needled conifers and small-leaved broadleaf evergreens can be sheared and still look presentable.

Heading usually results in lots of new growth spurting out just below the prune point. The many plants that are not well suited to this treatment will suffer if they are cut this way—interior leaves will die and not be replaced, and the plant will be stressed trying to grow new leaves.

Thinning involves cutting an entire branch off. This allows the gardener to improve the shape and structure of the shrub without overstimulating growth, and lets the plant grow into its natural shape. Thinning also prevents the plant from becoming too large for its space.

To my eye, a shrub pruned into a formal geometric shape is jarring. Few plants naturally feature 90 degree angles, perfectly straight sides, or conical tops. When you prune for shape, keep in mind the natural form of the plant.

TREES

 any gardeners overlook this entire group of plants when they design their gardens—this is a mistake, because there are lovely trees for almost every situation. Trees touch our hearts. They symbolize permanence, stability, and structure. Trees are the plants most likely to outlive the gardener who planted them. They are easy to grow, require little care after they become established, and are interesting and decorative all year 'round.

❧

Cutting the top off a mature tree may well result in the tree's death. If the tree does manage to survive, the topping off will only stimulate vigorous new growth, making it larger and more top-heavy than ever.

❧

When transplanting a bareroot tree, it is a sound practice to remove about a third of the top growth. A bareroot tree will have lost a lot of its root; even more importantly, most of its fine, hairlike feeder roots will have been destroyed by the process of digging it up and removing the soil from its roots. Cutting the top of the tree at this stage will not harm the tree.

TREES FOR SMALL GARDENS

In a small yard or a garden patio area, trees provide a focal point, a good starting place for the overall design of the area. What is needed in this sort of space is a friendly and well-behaved tree, one that is easy to live with up-close and personal. The tree should be free of problem pests and not subject to disease. When mature, it should be tall enough to walk under and substantial enough to provide some shade. The roots shouldn't heave pavement or invade planted areas. Showy flowers are a bonus, but on a patio or near a swimming pool fruit is an unwelcome feature. So is messy bark or a very heavy leaf drop.

Choice patio trees include small maples—trident, paperbark, amur, and many of the Japanese maples; redbud (*Cercis* spp.); the Japanese pagoda tree; some small magnolias; smaller dogwoods; and the Raywood ash (*Fraxinus angustifolia* 'Raywood'). Some plants usually thought of as shrubs, such as cornelian cherry dogwood and smoke tree, can be trained as small trees by removing side branches as they appear, encouraging a strong central trunk.

LARGER TREES

Trees that may reach 25 feet (7m) or so make excellent garden subjects. In warm areas, citrus trees are an excellent choice, and provide the bonus of delicious fruit and fragrant blossoms. Goldenchain (*Laburnum* spp.), with its yellow flowers like sweet peas, dresses up the garden and is widely adaptable. Make sure to trim off the suckers to maintain a single-trunked tree. There is a weeping cultivar called 'Pendulum'. Another great tree, one which should be planted more often, is *Koelreuteria*, known

as both the goldenrain tree and the Chinese lantern tree. It is reminiscent of goldenchain, but blooms later in the year, usually in midsummer.

Some of the best garden trees are the various flowering "fruitless" fruit trees—plum, peach, cherry, almond, and pear. While the flowering almond is almost always grown as a shrub, the others are trees with striking spring floral displays. These trees are all in the *Prunus* family. The selection is vast. Most of these flowering trees don't get above 20 feet (6m) tall, and many stay shorter. One of the most striking is *Prunus subhirtella* 'Yae-shidare-higan', the double weeping cherry. It is also one of the most widely adapted, growing in most areas except the warmest Pacific Coast states and the Deep South.

TALL TREES

If you have the space, larger trees can make a dramatic and memorable statement. Oaks (*Quercus* spp.), sycamores (*Platanus* spp.), and locusts (*Robinia* spp.) have many good-looking specimens. Don't overlook the evergreens, like cedars (*Cedrus* spp.) and pines (*Pinus* spp.).

A World Favorite—Eucalyptus

The eucalyptus is the most widely planted tree in the world. Vast tracts of eucalyptus in Africa, Asia, and South America, as well as in its native Australia, provide wood and pulp. These commercial plantations are planted with species too large to fit easily in home gardens, but there are lots and lots of eucalyptus varieties—it is the largest group of trees as well as the most widely planted.

With more than five hundred types, there is a eucalyptus for almost every garden in Zone 7 and south. Leaves may be round or long, spear-shaped or finely divided. Bark is hard, dark, and furrowed or white and smooth. There are stringybarks and ironbarks, and some eucalyptus with bark that flakes and peels, uncovering multicolored trunks. There are eucalyptus that look like willows and a few that smell like peppermint—one, *Eucalyptus nicholii*, has both of these features, and is called the willow-leafed peppermint.

Some weak-stemmed eucalyptus make good groundcovers. Other types, called mallees in Australia, are multitrunked shrubs. The Argyle apple (*Eucalyptus cinerea*) would look at home in a New England orchard. All tolerate light frost, and a few are hardy to 0°F (-17.7°C). Some love the desert, while others thrive in oceanside salt spray.

Tree Lore

While most trees are admired, even revered, as plants worthy of a special affection and devotion, some have another sort of reputation, at least in places.

The hawthorn is looked on by many as a cursed tree, bringing bad luck and unfortunate occurrences. The Missouri legislature named the hawthorn bloom as the state flower, but many people in the Ozarks won't touch one, and regard being in close proximity to a blooming hawthorn as potentially unlucky. Anthropologists who have studied the area and its people have been unable to determine the source of the belief, and it may well be fading today, but the hawthorn has long been an object of worry for many people of the region.

The redbud is sometimes called the Judas tree, since in folk belief Judas hanged himself on this tree in his remorse for betraying Jesus. The 1937 Oklahoma legislature named the redbud the state tree, stirring up what must have been an unexpected storm of controversy. Even a vice-president of the General Federation of Women's Clubs led a vigorous protest. The protest was based not only on the tree's supposed involvement with the betrayer Judas, but also by a belief that the blooming redbud is bewitched and a special occasion of danger after dark. Bewitched the redbud may be, but it wasn't the tree Judas used. *Cercis canadensis*, the commonly planted redbud of gardens, is native to North America.

There is, however, a redbud known as the Judas tree that is a native of southern Europe. This is the species *siliquastrum*, almost unknown in North America, and certainly not the subject of Oklahoma legislative notice.

An ancient practice designed to spur fruiting in a tree is to pound nails into the trunk. It doesn't work, of course, but the practice continues today.

HARVESTING TIPS

arvesting is the really easy part of gardening—just go ahead, pick or pull, and enjoy. There are some special things to know for those crops that will still be growing at the end of the season.

If you still have some beets in the ground in late autumn, you can try mulching them for later harvesting. While success isn't guaranteed, it might work, and pulling fresh beets from a snowy field is kind of fun.

Cabbage will spoil if it freezes, so harvest it before frost threatens. The best way to select heads for storage is to pick the ones that feel heavy for their size.

❧

Carrots can stay in the ground through the winter if your ground doesn't freeze solid. They should be protected with a mulch. Once picked, carrots will dry out quickly if the tops are left on, so cut them off, leaving an inch or two (2.5–5cm) of green.

❧

Make sure you have located and harvested all your potatoes before the ground freezes. They are ready to harvest when the tops die down. Leaving them in the ground for a couple of weeks longer toughens their skins, improving their storage qualities. Any left will probably winter over and sprout in the spring. There's nothing wrong with that, except potatoes should not be grown in the same area two years in a row, to lessen the possibility of disease.

❧

Pumpkins can begin to rot if left in contact with the ground. As they are ripening, put something between the pumpkin and the ground—a short length of board, a shingle, or anything else that will stay dry where it touches the pumpkin. Pumpkins are ready to pick when the vines wither. Cut the pumpkin away from the vine and leave a stem of 3 or 4 inches (7–10cm). Treat the pumpkins tenderly, since a break in the skin can lead to rot. If you store them for a while, don't wash them. Pumpkins can take light frosts in the field, but need to be protected from a hard freeze.

❧

Treat winter squash the same way you do pumpkins, above. Leaving a stem on is important, as squash and pumpkins will begin to rot without it.

❧

If you had a turnip planting fest in July, you don't need to harvest just yet. These vegetables can be left in the ground until it begins to freeze. But don't leave them too long. For best quality, pull turnips before they get too large. About 3 inches (7cm) in diameter is as big as you want them to grow.

❧

If you grow Brussels sprouts, remember that some light frost improves the flavor. If this is your first time growing them, you may have been surprised to see how they grow, held tight to the main stalk by a tiny stem. Pick from the bottom up, before the lower leaves turn yellow.

❧

Although collards are eaten mostly in the South, the plants are quite tolerant of frost. As with sprouts, the taste of collard greens is improved by a visit from Jack Frost.

❧

Onions should be harvested when most of the tops begin to dry and fall over. Once the bulbs are mature, pull them. If left in the soil at that stage they will rot. Allow the freshly pulled onions to dry in dappled sun for a couple of days, and then bring them into a protected area to dry for an additional several weeks. If you cut off the stems, leave several inches (7cm) on, or rot might set in. Allow them to dry with soil on them—once the onions are completely dry the soil will brush off easily. If some of your onions have thick necks, use them in the kitchen first, since they will store poorly.

GETTING READY FOR WINTER—AND SPRING

Y ou can take some important steps in the autumn to improve your gardening success the following year. Start by cleaning up the vegetable and annual flower areas after the harvest is completed. Pull all the weeds. If you have been good all through the year there won't be many left! If you still have some flowers that have gone to seed, you can leave those for the birds.

Don't leave discarded plant parts on the ground through the winter. Many insect pests will overwinter there, and they'll be all too ready to emerge in the spring. In alphabetical order, here are some of the insects that can overwinter in discarded vegetative matter: apple maggot, cabbage looper, cabbage worm, carrot rust fly, cheery fruit fly (related to the apple maggot), coddling moth, corn earworm, cutworms, European corn borer, fall armyworm, leafminers, Mexican bean beetle, onion maggot, plum curculio, squash bugs, tarnished plant bugs, and weevils. Many of these overwinterers can be reduced by tilling the soil, exposing the grubs to birds.

Tomato and melon vines are especially good harbors for next year's diseases and pests. If you are maintaining a compost pile, shred the vines and throw them in. If not, burn them if it's legal or dispose of them in plastic bags.

PLANTING COVER CROPS

One of the easiest ways to improve your soil's structure and add nutrients is to plant a cover crop in the autumn and till or dig it under in spring, about three or four weeks before planting out. Cover crops are simply a specialized type of green manure, a plant grown to be added directly back into the soil to enrich and improve it.

You can put a cover crop on small areas just as well as large ones. You don't need to have a whole field available to grow a cover crop. A 2-by-4-foot (60×120cm) bed benefits just as much as half an acre.

A cover crop cut in the spring and tilled in improves the soil by adding humus. Many gardeners, especially novices, are mystified by the term "humus." It's not all that mysterious. Humus is the decomposed remains of vegetable and animal matter. Anything that decomposes in the soil adds humus. Mostly, though, humus is the broken-down final product of animal or vegetable matter.

The best cover crop depends in large part on your winter weather. Winter wheat and annual rye are the best choices for very cold climates. Planted in the autumn before really cold weather comes, they will establish themselves before the ground freezes and grow rapidly once the weather warms up some in the spring. Hairy vetch, crimson clover, berseem clover, medic mix, and Austrian field peas are popular winter cover crops in warmer parts of the country.

I have had good success with crimson clover and vetch, both mowed after they flower but before they go to seed. They each add lots of organic matter, and both fix nitrogen. You can enhance the nitrogen-fixing abilities of legumes by treating the seeds or the soil with inoculants as you plant. Inoculants are available where you buy the seeds.

WINTER MULCHES

One of the best materials for mulching is leaves, either shredded or whole. Leaves are usually available in quantity in the autumn. Use your own, your neighbor's, or collect them from around the neighborhood. Leaves are much easier to handle if they are shredded by passing over them once or twice with a lawn mower.

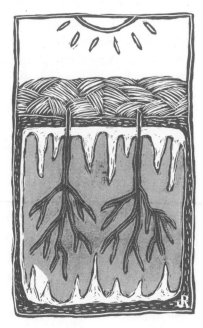

Three or 4 inches (7–10cm) of shredded leaves make a fine winter mulch for perennials or bulbs. Wait until the ground surface freezes, then cover it with the leaves.

Whole leaves tend to blow away unless they are in some sort of container. One old trick is to use inverted tomato cages around roses in the winter, stuffing them tightly with dry leaves. The cages should be inverted so the wider area is on the bottom.

Any organic mulch may be used in the winter, but mechanical ones such as black plastic should be reserved for the summer. Black plastic will make the soil too dry underneath them, and can also promote disease. If you have wood chips available, put them down in the winter and let them decay during the dormant season for the plants they are protecting. This way you don't need to use additional nitrogen, as you would during the growing season. Wood chips use soil nitrogen to help with the rotting process, but that nitrogen returns to the soil as the wood chips decompose.

Mulches can be used to cover bare soil in the winter, not just as plant protectors. If you don't grow a cover crop, try to cover the soil with shredded leaves or other organic material. Spoiled hay can be used, but you may have to till quickly in the spring to prevent grass or weed seeds contained in the hay from germinating.

PREPARING PLANTS FOR WINTER

Continue to enjoy carrots, beets, and other root crops you planted in the summer. If you had the foresight to put in some broccoli in August (and if it survived the extreme heat it may have encountered early), it should be just right to harvest now. Midseason plantings of cabbage are ready to pick late in the autumn. They will survive frost. Lettuce planted around Labor Day will be ready for Halloween salads. Some gardeners put in peas to harvest in the late autumn. Radishes, with their 30-days-to-harvest style, are a good autumn crop. There may still be some late-season flowers, especially asters.

GLADIOLI AND DAHLIAS

After you have a few light frosts it's time to lift and clean gladiolus corms and dahlia tubers. You can leave dahlias in the ground if you have excellent drainage and the ground does not freeze. Otherwise, dig them up carefully and let them dry for a day or two. Sometimes the old hollow stem remnants will have water in them, so leave the tubers to dry upside-down. The tubers need to be kept in a cool, dark place, but if they freeze they will die. The best practice is to put them in a box and cover with slightly damp vermiculite, perlite, or other neutral material, and cover them with plastic.

When you dig your gladioli for storage you will find evidence that the corms have spent most of the summer reproducing—the corms will be surrounded by little cormels. The original corm will have given its all and withered, replaced if you are lucky with a corm as large or larger. After digging, cut the foliage off, leaving no more than half an inch (1cm), and let the corms and cormels dry indoors for a couple of weeks. Then, separate the corms and cormels by size and store them in paper bags. An old trick to kill any thrips that may have settled in for a long winter's nap is to include a few moth flakes in the bag. You can also add a little of the bulb dust designed to prevent storage damage. Look for bulb dust that combines rotenone and sulfur.

In the spring all the little cormels can be planted and will grow into small plants, probably flowering in their second year. However, gladioli are so prolific that you may tire of this after a while and keep only the largest cormels, throwing away the rest.

DIVIDING PERENNIAL PLANTS

Autumn is the best time to divide most perennials (except those still in bloom). In general, it is beneficial to divide perennials every three or four years, to promote healthy vigor.

Before you actually divide perennials, prepare the new bed, loosening the soil and adding organic matter. Compost is good if you have it, but any organic matter will work. This is the very thing soil conditioners are made for. Also work in manure or an all-purpose, slow-acting fertilizer. Water the bed well.

To divide plants, dig up any that look crowded and pull roots apart, cutting them if necessary. Old foliage should be trimmed off, leaving several inches (7cm) on evergreen plants. Most perennial roots have visible growing points, so make sure each piece includes some. Growth points will be pointing upward.

Replant the divided roots. Most should be covered with 3 or 4 inches (7–10cm) of soil. Peonies are an exception. Never bury them more than 2 inches (5cm) deep—if they are planted more deeply flowering will be greatly delayed. Two inches never seems to be enough to me. It is, though, so don't try to protect peony roots with a heavier blanket of soil.

If you garden in an area where the ground freezes, protect your perennials with a generous covering of mulch. Four to 6 inches (10–15cm) of mulch is not too much, applied after the first hard freeze. The mulch is intended to maintain an even soil temperature and prevent damage to plants from freeze-thaw cycles.

Among the perennials that profit from autumn division are daylilies, oriental poppies, artemisia, gaillardia, Shasta daises, primroses, iris, peonies, salvia, perennial phlox, many sedums, and astilbes.

One tip—ornamental grasses respond best when divided in the spring. They don't recover well when they are pruned as the temperatures are dropping.

TOOL CARE AND STORAGE

CARING FOR HAND TOOLS AND GARDEN ACCESSORIES

 efore you put your garden tools away for the winter, be sure to clean them well. All dirt should be washed off. Spades and hoes may be sharpened with a file. Clean up and sharpen pruners and loppers. Clean dirt off hand tools such as trowels and cultivators.

While you should store your tools in a dry place over the winter, many storage areas such as sheds and basements are damp by nature. Rust prevention treatment is therefore good insurance that your tools will be in fine shape come spring. WD-40 or light machine oil can be used to rustproof metal surfaces. If you are draining oil from power equipment, you can make an effective rust preventer from a rag dipped in the old oil. Just wipe metal parts with the rag and wipe off the excess, leaving a thin film of oil.

Wooden and metal stakes, tomato cages (other than those protecting your roses), and other small garden accessories should be cleaned and put away in a dry place.

Clean push lawn mowers, getting rid of dried grass with a stiff wire brush. An oily rag can be used on the reel blades to prevent rust. If you want to be really organized, sharpen the mower blades now rather than waiting for spring.

Flush and drain irrigation systems. If you leave the irrigation pipes and hoses in place, seal off the ends. A plastic sandwich bag secured with a twist tie does this nicely. Drain hoses after removing nozzles and sprinklers, and bring them in out of the weather.

POWER EQUIPMENT SHUT DOWN

If your mower or other gasoline-powered equipment will not be used for an extended period, there are storage procedures you should follow. Gasoline can turn gummy, so all gasoline should be drained from the fuel system. The easiest way is to let the engine run until it's out of gas. So, as you near the beginning of the storage period, add just a little gas at a time—don't fill the tank.

❧

If you don't want to drain your gas tank, you can use an additive that will allow long-term storage. (Note that if your gasoline contains alcohol, it MUST ALL be removed from the engine and tank.)

❧

Drain the oil from the crankcase when the engine and oil are warm. Remove the spark plug, and add an ounce of oil to the cylinder. Replace the plug and run the engine briefly and slowly to distribute the oil. Clean off all dirt, grass bits, and crud from the engine area.

❧

142

Any batteries for power equipment should be disconnected and stored in a cold place, such as a garage.

❧

Rub rust-prone surfaces with a cloth dipped in a light oil, or spray with a silicone rust proofer.

❧

Rotary mowers—riding, gas, or electric—will have a crust of dried grass lining their deck undersides, and this must be scraped off. Drain and replace oil. Follow directions in your owner's manual for winterizing gasoline engines.

GIFT PLANTS AND THEIR CARE

AMARYLLIS

One of the most popular Christmas gift plants is amaryllis. (See also Forcing Bulbs in Containers on page 104.) This plant is easy to care for all through the year and, when given good conditions, will flower year after year. Usually the flower stalk appears first, and is followed by broad, deep green leaves. The flower stalk will grow rapidly, reaching 2 feet (60cm) or more above the pot. Buds appear, usually four, pointing to the four primary compass points. They will open one at a time, and individual blossoms from the largest bulbs can grow to as much as eight inches (20cm) across. Large bulbs may produce a second flower stalk, usually somewhat smaller than the first, but still impressive.

As the flower begins to fade, pick it off, leaving most of the stalk to die back. That stalk, ugly as it may seem, is sending a lot of food into the bulb, which is pretty well wiped out after producing the bloom you were so crazy about. You can twist the stalk off after it turns pale and begins to dry up. Water occasionally, but let the top of the mix dry out

before adding more water. With each watering, include a balanced liquid fertilizer at half-strength.

❧

Give your amaryllis as much light as you can. It's a warm-weather native, and won't tolerate frost, so keep the plant indoors until all danger of frost has abated. Once the weather is reliably warm, move your amaryllis outside, but take care because the leaves will burn if direct sunlight hits them for any length of time at first. This is true even if you had the plant in a very sunny window indoors. The first day give your amaryllis half an hour of direct sun; the second day increase the time to an hour; add about half an hour of time in the sun each day until the plant is able to tolerate a day of full sun after a week or ten days.

Once my amaryllis has become accustomed to being an outdoor plant, and against all conventional gardening advice, I plant it in the garden, in the richest soil I have. I leave it there until the first hard frost, which will kill back the leaves. The I dig it up and bring it indoors, and set it in a cool quiet place. At this time I trim off any leaves still left, and let the bulb sleep for a month or two. Finally, I shake off any old dirt, pull away any roots that have gone completely flat and brown, and repot it in the best potting soil I can buy. It is important to use a pot only slightly larger than the bulb and root mass, since amaryllis blooms best when crowded.

To repot the plant properly, fill the bottom third of the pot with soil and place the bulb on top of it. Then fill soil in around the bulb, leaving a third to a half of the bulb above the potting mix. Be sure to gently push soil between the roots so that no air holes remain. Tapping the pot sharply on the bench or ground helps to settle the soil. Water well, and place the plant in a warm, bright room. Don't water again until growth starts. The flower stalk usually emerges first. If all you get is leaves, the bulb did not restore enough energy after it bloomed, and will bloom next year. Just let it grow in as much light as possible, since good light is key to future performance.

GLOXINIA

Another popular plant for gift-giving is the florist gloxinia. Related to African violets, the gloxinia is prized for its large flowers that come in almost every color except green. The proper name of this plant is *Sinningia*, but everyone refers to it as gloxinia. A botanist would insist that gloxinia is the proper name only for a species related to the Gesneria family, but that is a distinction important chiefly to specialists.

I have a friend who once received a gloxinia as a present and proudly displayed it on her desk at work. I was in her office one day, and asked where the gloxinia was. Oh, she told me, it died, so I threw it out. I didn't have the heart to tell her that, most likely, it had not died but had gone dormant, as gloxinias naturally do.

After a long period of spectacular floral display, the gloxinia will lose its blossoms and the leaves will start to become dry and yellow. Don't worry, the plant is only doing what comes naturally. The worst thing you can do at this point, aside from pitching it, is to think it needs water, and soak it. Instead, set it aside for two or three weeks without watering. Then trim off the withering foliage and bring the pot back into a warm, sunny place near a window and water it a bit, but again, don't soak. Sometimes it is recommended that you set the plant aside for several months, but this is bad advice. In that case, the tuber will most likely dry out completely, and the plant really will die.

When you see new leaves beginning to sprout from the tuber, it's time to repot. Use good potting soil and a clean (or cleaned) pot. The new leaves will grow slowly, and new roots will be forming under the surface. The normal bloom time for gloxinia is mid- to late summer.

EASTER LILIES

Legend has it that beautiful white lilies sprang up where drops of Christ's tears fell in the Garden of Gethsemane. Even if this charming legend is true, the flower we call the Easter lily didn't spring up in the Holy Land; rather, it is a native of Japan. Easter lilies were imported in large quantities from Japan until the advent of World War II. When the supply was cut off an American source was developed, concentrated in a narrow band of coastal land on the Oregon-California border.

Easter lilies are popular gift plants, and can successfully be made a part of your outdoor garden using a few simple procedures. The Easter lily you received as a gift was probably forced into bloom for Easter by manipulating the plant's growing environment to resemble summer, the flower's normal bloom period.

Keep your potted lily watered and fed, using a regular houseplant fertilizer. Plant it out in the garden in well-drained soil, after all danger of frost has passed. Lilies like to grow in the sun, but should have their roots in cool ground, a situation that calls for mulch. In cold climates the plant should be mulched heavily to protect it from winter chill. The lily may rebloom the autumn after it was planted, but most likely it will take a year or two to recover from the forcing process, and then bloom in midsummer.

One note of caution: Forced lilies shouldn't be planted anywhere near other lilies, since they may carry and transmit a virus called the mosaic virus, for which there is no treatment or cure.

AZALEA

An azalea makes a pretty gift plant, but indoor conditions tend to make it unhappy. You can keep a small potted azalea inside until the blossoms start to fade and drop off, and then return it to the great out-doors. While inside the azalea should be watered well. If the weather outside is cold, it should be moved gradually, so it can reacclimate itself to outdoor conditions. An enclosed unheated porch or garage makes an ideal temporary staging area. It should be planted into the ground, with proper notice taken of its need for acidic soil conditions, as soon as the ground can be worked in the spring.

HOUSEPLANT CARE

WATERING YOUR PLANTS

ater about half as often as you think is necessary. The primary cause of houseplant problems is too much care and attention, I think, and especially too much water, followed closely by too much fertilizer. Particularly in the winter, houseplants don't require a lot of water. Many of them slow their growth dramatically in the winter, taking it easy for the season. Since they aren't doing much growing, they don't need much water. A general rule of thumb is to let the top inch or two (2.5–5cm) of soil get dry to the touch before watering again.

Houseplants do get dusty, and like to be hosed off. For most plants this is easy enough to accomplish. Simply put them in the bathtub and turn the shower on. Or set them in the tub or sink and water the plants with an old-fashioned shampoo or dish-rinsing attachment, which can be set to make a soft spray. Even African violets can have a bath as long as the water is lukewarm (make it close to room temperature). Cold water will spot African violet leaves permanently.

Indoor air in winter is far too dry for most plants. To raise the humidity around houseplants, place them on trays filled with pebbles and add water to the trays. The pots should rest on the pebbles, not in the water. Aquarium gravel can make an attractive bed. Note that misting the air has a very short-lived effect.

FEEDING HOUSEPLANTS

Fertilize houseplants when they are starting into a growth cycle. For most houseplants, this is in the spring. Apply fertilizer at half the recommended strength, and fertilize every time you water. Occasionally water heavily, so the excess water runs out of the bottom of the pot and flushes away excess fertilizer salts.

THE RIGHT LIGHT

Most houseplants like to summer outdoors. Avoid a lot of direct sunlight, since many houseplants are tropical natives that grew in jungles, and the jungle floor has low light.

During the time the plants are in the house, provide as much natural light as possible. Very few plants will grow well in an artificially lit atmosphere—at least some natural light is needed.

For plants that flower or have brightly colored

leaves, the more light the better. If you have your plants in a sunny window, turn them a quarter turn every day so that they don't grow lopsided. If they don't get a quarter turn every day, it's not fatal, but do remember to turn them regularly.

FACING YOUR MISTAKES

utumn is the time to bite the bullet and take out plants that haven't worked for whatever reason. Gardening is about change; no garden is ever finished. It's best to acknowledge reality, remove a mistake, and spend the winter visualizing the great new plant you now have space for.

Sometimes a plant just won't grow well. The climate is favorable, you prepared the soil properly, watering and feeding were done properly, the light was right, but no matter. The plant just didn't grow the way it should, and seems sickly or sulky. Dig it up and toss it. Be decisive. Space is precious in a garden, and you don't have room for a plant that isn't happy.

If a plant fails to thrive, the mistake may very well be yours. Perhaps you put a good plant in a bad place. You didn't check out the light requirements. You forgot how boggy that corner gets in spring, though you knew the plant required excellent drainage. Or maybe it wasn't oversight. Maybe you just wanted that plant in that space so much you tried to force it. Well, sometimes that works, but sometimes it doesn't. Remove your mistakes in autumn, while you are cleaning up and getting ready for the new year.

SOURCES

Listed below are reliable sources I have used to order high-quality plants and seeds. These sources all handle high-quality merchandise and take good care of their customers. First, though, patronize your local garden centers and nurseries. Their plants will be suitable for your area, and will already be adjusted to local conditions.

SEEDS

The Cook's Garden
P.O. Box 535
Londonderry, VT 05148
800 457-9703
Catalog free.
Excellent selection of lettuce and salad greens seeds, other vegetables. Some flower seeds, preserving supplies.

J. L. Hudson, Seedsman
P.O. Box 1058
Redwood City, CA 94064
No telephone
Catalog address only, Catalog $1.00
Fascinating collection of seeds rare and common, all open-pollinated. Catalog is a treasure of horticultural information. Source for chia-type Salvia seeds.

Johnny's Selected Seeds
1 Foss Hill Road
RR 1, Box 2580
Albion, ME 04910-9731
207 437-4301
Catalog free.
Large selection of vegetable and flower seeds, together with ground cover and green manures, tools, and books.

Park Seed
1 Parkton Ave.
Greenwood, SC 29647-0001
800 845-3369
Catalog free.
Traditional seed supplier, wide selection of vegetable and flower seeds and supplies. Source for Frithia (listed under succulents). Also sells some plants and bulbs.

Territorial Seed Co.
P.O. Box 157
Cottage Grove, OR 97424
541 942-9547
Catalog free
Specializes in seeds for the maritime Northwest. Excellent selection. Spring and Fall catalogs, lists some bulbs and supplies.

Wildseed Farms
P.O. Box 3000
Fredericksburg, TX 78624-3000
800 848-0078
Catalog free.
Good selection of wildflower seeds. Catalog provides extensive advice on planting and germination.

PLANTS

Filaree Farms
182 Conconully Highway
Okanogan, WA 98840
509 422-6940
Catalog $2.00.
Garlic specialists.

Forestfarm
990 Tetherow Rd.
Williams, OR 97544-9599
541 846-7269
Catalog $4.00.
*Unsurpassed array of woody plants,
    perennials, grasses, and ferns.
    You may well find here what you
    have looked for unsuccessfully for
    a long time.*

Nichols Garden Nursery
1190 North Pacific Highway
Albany, OR 97321-4580
541 928-9280
Catalog free.
*Specializes in herbs, both plants and seeds.
    Also carries vegetable and flower seeds,
    herbal teas, herbs and spices, and
    essential oils. Interesting catalog,
    family-run business.*

Northwoods Nursery
27635 S. Oglesby Rd.
Canby, OR 97013
503 266-5432
Catalog free.
*Medicinal plants, unusual fruits, and
    ornamentals.*

Ronniger's Seed and Potato Co.
P.O. Box 307
Ellensburg, WA 98926
800 846-6178
Catalog free.
*Mostly potatoes, wide selection of standard
    and special varieties. Also some alliums,
    fruits, asparagus, and green manures.*

John Scheepers, Inc.
Van Engelen, Inc.
23 Tulip Drive
Bantam, CT 06750
800 567-0838 (Scheepers)
800 567-8734 (Van Engelen)
Catalogs free.
*Bulb suppliers. Scheepers is the retail side of
    the business, while Van Engelen sells in
    large quantities, usually by the hundred.
    Scheepers has a slightly larger selection,
    and some of its bulbs are slightly larger
    than Van Engelen's, but both companies
    supply superior merchandise. These are
    the people to see for large quantities of
    mainstream bulbs. They feature a good
    selection of amaryllis, including ones
    especially prepared to bloom at
    Christmas. They also carry lilies.*

Siskiyou Rare Plant Nursery
2825 Cummings Rd.
Medford, OR 97501
541 772-6846
Catalog $3.00.
*A superb collection of unusual plants,
    especially those for the rock garden,
    dwarf conifers, ferns, Japanese maples,
    and ornamental grasses.*

Wayside Gardens
1 Garden Lane
Hodges, SC 29695-0001
888 234-7136
Catalog free.
*Very comprehensive catalog of ornamental
plants, some bulbs. Some rare (and
expensive) plants not found elsewhere.*

White Flower Farms
P.O. Box 50
Litchfield, CT 06759-0050
800 411-6159
Catalog free.
*Wide selection of garden ornamentals,
very detailed information on plants.
Unusual varieties.*

CANADIAN SOURCES

Corn Hill Nursery Ltd.
RR 5
Petitcodiac NB EOA 2HO

Ferncliff Gardens
SS 1
Mission, British Columbia
V2V 5V6

McFayden Seed Co. Ltd.
Box 1800
Brandon, Manitoba
R7A 6N4

Stirling Perennials
RR 1
Morpeth, Ontario
N0P 1X0

AUSTRALIAN SOURCES

Country Farm Perennials
RSD Laings Road
Nayook VIC 3821

Cox's Nursery
RMB 216 Oaks Road
Thrilmere NSW 2572

Honeysuckle Cottage Nursery
Lot 35 Bowen Mountain Road
Bowen Mountain via Grosevale
NSW 2753

Swan Bros Pty Ltd
490 Galston Road
Dural NSW 2158

Garden Knowledge

If there is a public garden, university botanic garden, arboretum, or anything of that nature near you, become a member. There is no better place to get solid information on plants and gardening, information which will be tailored for your climate and growing conditions. Sales of unusual and desirable plants are often held, and sometimes short courses on gardening and horticulture are presented, often at little or no cost. And there is a bonus—you'll meet the nicest people.

In addition to local institutions, I'd recommend a membership in the Brooklyn Botanic Garden. BBG sends to members a quarterly book, about 120 pages, each on a different topic. Taken together and saved over the years these books form almost an encyclopedia of garden information. Memberships begin at $35.00 a year, and if you live in the Brooklyn area you receive benefits in addition to the books. But the books themselves make membership worthwhile, even for a gardener like me who lives on the opposite side of the country. More expensive membership entitles you to a free plant or two from the Garden's collection, often something unusual.

Membership Department
Brooklyn Botanic Garden
1000 Washington Ave.
Brooklyn, NY 11225-1099

BIBLIOGRAPHY

Abraham, Doc and Katy. *Green Thumb Wisdom*. Pownal, Vermont: Storey Communications, 1996.

Baker, Margaret. *Gardener's Magic and Folklore*. New York: Universe Books, 1978.

Brooklyn Botanic Garden Record, various authors. (Brooklyn Botanic Garden, quarterly)

Randolph, Vance. *Ozark Magic and Folklore*. New York: Dover, 1964.

Riotte, Louise. *Astrological Gardening*. Pownal, Vermont: Storey Communications, 1989.

————. *Sleeping With a Sunflower*. Pownal, Vermont: Storey Communications, 1987.

Swain, Roger. *The Practical Gardener*. Boston: Little, Brown, 1989.

Stout, Ruth. *Gardening Without Work*. New York: Devon-Adair, 1961.

Sunset National Garden Book. Menlo Park, California: Sunset Books, 1997.

INDEX

OLD-FASHIONED
GARDEN WISDOM

Designed by Jennifer S. Markson
and set in Goudy and Goudy Handtool.
Illustrated by Joanna Roy.
Color separations by Colourscan Overseas Co. Pte Ltd.
Printed by Midas Printing Limited
on an acid-free paper.